Subliminal

by

Lee M. Shulman, Ph.D.
Joyce Shulman, Ph.D.
Gerald P. Rafferty

Library of Congress Cataloging in Publications Data
Shulman, Lee M.
Subliminal: The New Channel to Personal
Power.
1. Psychology — Case studies. 2. Self-
actualization (Psychology) — Case studies.
2. I. Shulman, Joyce. II. Rafferty, Gerald P.
III. Title.
89-82770
ISBN 0-931137-14-4

Published by InfoBooks
P. O. Box 1018, Santa Monica, CA 90406

© 1990 InfoBooks
All rights reserved. No part of this book may be
reproduced, in any form or by any means, without permission in writing from the publisher.

Cover and text illustrations: Gloria Garland

Printed in the United States of America

10 9 8 7 6 5 4 3 2 1

INFO
BOOKS
P.O. Box 1018
Santa Monica
California 90406
(213)-394-4102
Fax - 394-2603
1-800-669-0409

Subliminal

The New Channel to Personal Power

Contents

Acknowledgments Δ ix
Foreword Δ xvii

Chapter 1
Background to Subliminals Δ 1
Chapter 2
Subliminals All Around Us Δ 11
Chapter 3
Technical Notes Δ 31
Chapter 4
Psychology of Subliminals Δ 49
Chapter 5
Temporary or Permanent Δ 77
Chapter 6
The Power of the Mind Δ 87
Chapter 7
Subliminal Scripts Δ 99
Chapter 8
The Sounds of Subliminals Δ 123

Chapter 9
Testing Subliminals Δ 135
Chapter 10
Subliminals and the Law Δ 155
Chapter 11
The Future of Subliminals Δ 177

Appendix A
Subliminals for Weight Loss Δ 185
Appendix B
The Institute for Subliminal Studies Δ 209
Appendix C
Manufacturers and Their Products Δ 211
Appendix D
References and Further Reading Δ 215
Appendix E
Bibliography Δ 247

Index Δ 253

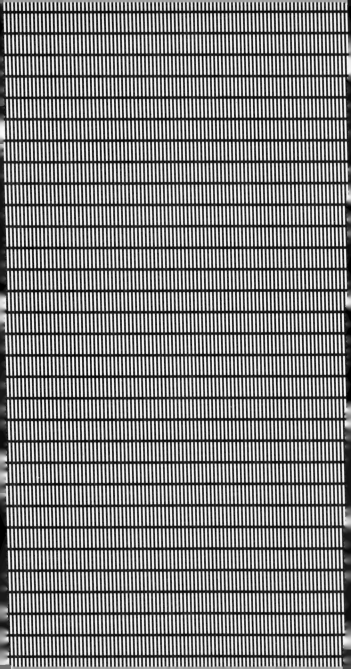

Acknowledgments

Acknowledgments are wonderful. What a great phrase, "I acknowledge you." It says so much. "I see you. I accept you. I like my connection with you. I thank you for being you and for choosing to include me in your life."

Acknowledgments are a smile. A nod. A loving wink. They're a tip of the hat. A thumbs- up. A job well done. A thank-you.

Happily and joyously, we, the authors, acknowledge each other. We had fun writing this book. The research was fascinating. Every new article and report we read opened up more new thoughts, new ideas, new directions, new places where we could lift the edges and peek to see what we could find. We thank the many brave and inventive scientists who boldly stepped into the unknown to create experiments and tests to study the subject of subliminal learning and then put in the time and effort to write up their work.

Acknowledgments Δ x

Our work wasn't all reading, not by far. We worked with many real, live people and they were great. They were thoroughly interested in this tantalizing subject and in our efforts to discover some truth about it. They cooperated by attending workshops we ran and trying the tapes we suggested. It would be quite impossible to list all of you individually. But we thanked you personally at the time we worked together, and we thank you again now as a group.

Quite a few people played larger roles in our work, and we'd like to thank some of you again here. We were most fortunate to have nine people, professionals and experts in their fields, read our manuscript and generously provide us with their criticisms and suggestions.

Norman Cousins, author and medical researcher and lecturer, read our manuscript and graciously offered to write a foreword for our book. Then he read the manuscript again, after revisions, and added a few just-right words to the foreword and tons more support and encouragement.

xi △ Acknowledgments

Nathaniel Branden, Ph.D., author of twelve books and tape programs on the psychology of self-esteem, also read the manuscript twice (before and after revisions) and gave us some excellent suggestions, which we followed, and much support and encouragement, which we appreciate.

Gershon Lesser, medical doctor, lawyer, medical editor for KCRW National Public Radio, also read the manuscript twice and was very generous with his suggestions and comments. We're delighted that you liked the work so much more the second time around, Gershon.

Feris M. Greenberger, lawyer, made intelligent and insightful comments and suggestions that greatly improved our efforts. No, Feris, we don't think you were being too picky. We appreciate your valuable help.

Joan Kennedy Taylor, is a writer and editor whose professional attention to our work gave us new insight. You not only reflected back to us what the book was, Joan, you helped us see what it could be. The book is longer (and we hope better) because of you. Thanks.

Larry Gottlieb is another writer whose careful reading of the manuscript uncovered those little, hidden things only another writer would find.

Gloria Garland, art director (she did the cover and art for this book), and Nancy Gordon, counselor, each agreed to read the manuscript from the fresh and open viewpoint of someone interested in, yet new to, the subject. Your suggestions were most helpful. If you read the book through again, you'll find where your comments created changes — hopefully for the better.

Other people contributed their expertise. We'd like to thank Jerry Gillies, author and lecturer, who rejuvenated our interest in subliminal tapes by bringing over samples of tapes he was sure really worked and by his boundless enthusiasm. We thank Dr. Alex Kirzhner, who is one of the leaders in the field of developing new and improved subliminal products. We thank you, Alex, for sharing so much of your expertise and your warm, Russian energy with us. We thank Susannah Lippman and Gordon Pierce of Alphasonics for sharing their extensive knowledge of the subject of subliminal tapes with us.

Many people contributed to our work, over time and space, through their printed works. We read many books, not only by the authors we've just mentioned in this section but by others, especially Dr. John Diamond, Dr. Roger Callahan, Dr. Milton Erickson, and Dr. Abraham Maslow.

We had help in our research. The extensive listing in the References and Further Reading section — Appendix D — would not have been possible without the diligent and creative efforts of Peter Derycz and Bill Bergman of Infotrieve Systems in Los Angeles, a computer search company that can, and did for us, access database files all around the world for current information on subliminal learning.

Others were there for us, with quiet strength. Nancy Brodsky helped with research, reading, and support. Joe Aidlin helped with legal guidance. The Inside Edge Group of Los Angeles helped by providing spiritual energy and enthusiasm. We'd like to extend the handshake of thanks back in time a bit to the places where we launched our academic pursuits: Wayne State University, University of Michigan, Walden University, and City University of New York.

A most important contributor is Shelley Mahr, our copyeditor. Shelley, you bravely ventured deep into the tangled underbrush of syntax and grammar and did a truly professional job of cleaning away the dead leaves and branches and trimming and pruning and moving and adjusting until each section could hold its head high to the light of readership. You did such a good job that your work is invisible. The reader will never know you were there; but we know and we acknowledge you and we appreciate you and we thank you.

And that brings us back to us, the authors.

Books last a long time and they're wonderful, cherished possessions. But we got more than a book out of all of our work. We developed a friendship; an open, accepting, trusting friendship that will last. We worked through those moments that all cooperative work relationships face, and we worked through them with an open ease and acceptance and trust that strengthened our bonds. Our weekly business meetings became warm and loving breakfast parties where we shared oats and bran and rice and fruit and tea and smiles and hugs. A year and a half ago we each, very seriously, checked our personal calenders and put effort into "setting aside an hour for a Friday meeting." Now we carefully guard our precious Friday mornings and other people get scheduled around them. And when we miss a Friday! The week just feels all wrong.

Our friendship reached a peak just a few weeks ago when we each agreed to go "where few co-authors have gone before" — on to another book together. In fact, it will be a book series. Perhaps it's not too surprising that the new books will be about relationships — how to tend them and nurture them in a busy and frantic world that seems to care very little about the joys and benefits of relationships. The first book in the new series will be called *The 30-Day Renewable Marriage — Keeping Romance Alive*. Drop us a line. We'll keep you posted.

Finally, we acknowledge you, our reader. You have been with us from the beginning, sitting just behind and a little to the right of the computer. You're the person we wrote the book for. Your smiles encouraged us to continue. Your frowns told us: "Wait a minute. Is that really true? Could you do some more research on that point, please?" You kept us on track by your gentle nudging: "Tell me something I don't know but I'd like to know. I'm a busy person with many demands on my time, so tell me what you're going to tell me clearly, plainly, truthfully. And, please, try to make it interesting."

You were with us when we began the book and you're with us now. We thank you for being there. We hope we served you well.

Foreword

Nothing in the universe is more fascinating, more compelling or complex, than the workings of the human mind. In recent years, ways have been developed of bypassing the conscious intelligence in order to promote susceptibility to ideas and viewpoints and even products. This "subliminal process" is rapidly becoming a substantial industry. It is being used as a powerful aid in learning, as a therapeutic tool in treating disorders, in banishing phobias of one sort or another, and as a way of insinuating advertising messages into the human mind without having to penetrate the barrier of the critical intelligence. The implications of all these approaches need not be underlined.

One of the deepest questions to confront human speculation is whether the human species is capable of ever higher levels of creative capability. Men such as Thomas Jefferson, John Adams, and Benjamin Franklin believed in the perfectibility of human beings. At a time when the problems of human survival are not only more complex but more insistent than ever before, it is essential to develop and nurture human capacity to its fullest.

Joyce and Lee Shulman and Gerald Rafferty have addressed themselves to techniques for extending the human mind. They have provided, in their thorough study of subliminal learning, a long-overdue examination of the ways of potentiating human beings. Against the background of the Shulmans' work in psychotherapy, they have scrutinized the benefits and hazards involved in the techniques by which the human subconscious can be penetrated. They have evaluated the entire field of subliminal tapes now available to the general public — an important service for people who have no way otherwise to judge the value of the multitude of offerings, from aids to peaceful slumber to mastery of foreign languages. Not the least of the book's fine qualities is the excellence of presentation. The writing is lucid and sequential and makes for a rewarding reading experience.

— Norman Cousins

Subliminal

The New Channel to Personal Power

Symbols: The triangle is an ancient symbol representing creative intellect, the Godhead, wisdom, and behavior. The inverted 'Y' represents wisdom or power coming from above to below. We combined these two ideas into one symbol and used it as marker throughout this book.

Background to Subliminals

Subliminal tapes represent some of the latest efforts, in a long line of efforts, to create tools, techniques, and methods whereby human beings can help themselves cope with the realities and mysteries of life, with the realities and mysteries of themselves.

History shows that human beings, almost from their first moments of being conscious, of being self-aware, have been striving to answer such questions as From whence have we come? Why are we here? and Where are we going? These questions have usually taken people to the outer edges of philosophy, metaphysics, and religion.

There are other questions which are constantly nudging us. Why do we do the things we do? Why do we think the thoughts we think? Is there anything we can do to change the way we do things? Is there anything we can do to change the way we think? If there are things we can do, what are they? How can we make them a part of ourselves? How can we change ourselves? And here we find the seed of the art and science of psychology.

For a long time, with the exception of a handful of outstanding thinkers — the few, the proud, the brave — it seems human beings pretty much accepted the idea that they were born to live out their lots in life. They followed the dictums of their Gods or their leaders or simply lived out the genetic inheritance of their parents. Life on this planet is tough and belief systems like these helped to keep a certain order to things.

We needed to survive as a species and a certain nonquestioning discipline was perhaps helpful and in order. Not so long ago life expectancy was half what it is today. People died early of illness and accidents and disease. There wasn't much time for self-examination and self-improvement programs. Perhaps more to the point, the prevailing belief was that our lives were dictated by forces beyond our control. We were who we were. We were destined to do what we did. And there wasn't much thought that we, as individuals, could ever do anything about it.

Yet, through the ages we see a single string which carried a whispered wisdom hinting that we each had within us all the power we needed to effect whatever changes we desired within ourselves or the world around us. Plutarch, an early Roman historian, credits Plato with the saying "Know thyself." (This powerful phrase is attributed to quite a few people: Pythagoras, Chilo, Thales, Cleobulus, Bias, Solon, and Socrates.) "Know thyself." A wonderful thought. Not only does it command us to the noble act of self-study, it implies that we are capable of it. This was perhaps the first hint that we possessed a channel to personal power.

Epictetus, a Roman philosopher in the first century A.D., gave us two more powerful hints to answer the questions Why do I do what I do? and How can I change?

"The appearance of things to the mind is the standard of every action to man." Giving us the hint that our thoughts precede our actions. "Men are disturbed not by things, but by the views which they take of them." Giving us the hint that our estimates, our thoughts about life's happenings, are more important in determining how we act, how we respond to life, than the happenings themselves.

This wisdom was passed, hand to hand, like a gleaming jewel in the relay race of history. The suggestion was there and it was clear: many of the answers to the questions we had about ourselves could be found within us. If, indeed, we are capable of knowing our actions by simple observation (and our actions are preceded by our thoughts), could we somehow know our thoughts? Could our thoughts observe themselves? Where do our thoughts come from? If they come from us, could we replace them with newer, better thoughts? Could we create new thoughts? And how do we do that? Could we give another person new thoughts and thereby change their actions? Could we change our own actions by changing our own thoughts?

Sigmund Freud was perhaps the first to suggest that the answers to the problems of the mentally ill were deep within the minds of the patients themselves. And he developed a means, a method, whereby he hoped to get inside the patient's mind and make adjustments to the patient's thinking so that the patient's behavior would change. Since then there have been hundreds of methods proposed to help people get inside of each other — therapist to patient — and effect change. From about the 1950s on, we have had the so-called self-help movement, where hundreds of new methods have been suggested to enable people to get inside of their own minds and make the adjustments and effect their own changes.

Lots of tools have come along: Psychoanalysis. Hypnosis. Self-Hypnosis. Group Therapy. Gestalt Therapy. Behaviorism. Psychodrama. Meditation. Affirmations. And now we have, with all the bells and whistles of modern technology, a tool called Subliminal Learning, subliminal behavior change.

This book is about subliminal learning. Is subliminal learning effective? Can we use subliminal tapes to really create desired change in our lives? Can subliminal tools be integrated into a person's overall growth program? And if so, how?

We see subliminal tapes as a current tool offered in a long line of tools designed to help individuals interact with themselves and become the people they have chosen to be.

We wrote this book to help answer the question of just how effective subliminal tapes are or could be. We enjoyed researching the subject and writing the book. We approached the subject with enthusiasm, healthy skepticism, and open-mindedness. As with any new subject, we expected to find controversy. We were not disappointed. There is controversy enough to satisfy the probing diligence of any investigator. Opinions span the entire spectrum from fear and suspicion and negativism all the way to outrageous claims that almost match the arm waving and shouting of a Bible-thumping hallelujah prayer meeting. Tangled someplace amid the fear and the noise, we hoped to find some truth. We think we did find some truth and we share it with you in this book.

Our studies were filled with living drama, the stuff of life.

A woman worked with subliminal tapes to lose over sixty pounds. With her new, sleek body she found a new, confident self who was able to do all the other work needed to rejuvenate the romance in her threatened marriage and return, with joy and enthusiasm, to a career she'd abandoned years before.

A man came to therapy bent and tired from years of living with a woman who physically, verbally, and emotionally abused him. He agreed to include subliminal tapes as a part of his overall therapy program. Within a few weeks the changes on his face and in his body were remarkable. He talked about himself and *his* needs. He announced, with verbal force and lively, quick hand gestures, what *he* expected for and from himself after the divorce. At the end of one session he glided out of the office, head held high and whistling some perky tune. The memory still wets the eyes.

We found drama too real for fiction. We found scientists hurling their research reports at each other like gauntlets from outraged knights. We found the dry, ever-so-neccessary, nitpicking analysis of scientists performing double-blind experiments, tweaking and adjusting their machines and protecting the day's results in hushed secrecy until the entire experiment was concluded. We found manufacturers of tapes apparently willing to promise that their tapes could help you do just about anything you could imagine. We found other manufacturers whose care and diligence impressed and reassured us. We found reports of tapes being used on unknowing audiences — shoppers in department stores, patients and visitors at hospital clinics. In short, we found it all.

We set out to see for ourselves if subliminal tapes were or could be a new channel to personal power. We think we found some special insights and promises, and it's our joy to share them with you. Let us begin.

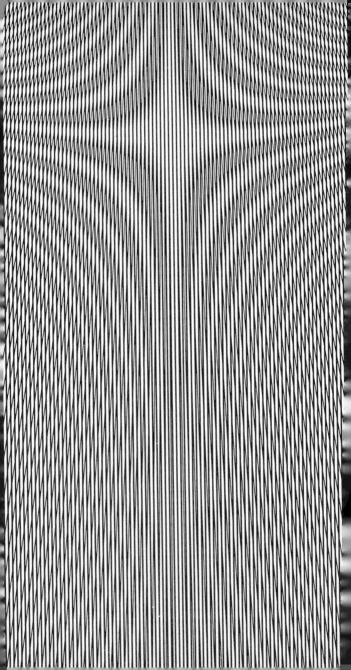

2
Subliminals All Around Us

We decided to write this book almost two years ago. As with most good decisions, this one came out of necessity.

Allow us to introduce ourselves. Two of the coauthors of this book, Lee and Joyce Shulman, are practicing psychologists and have always been at least open to the idea that subliminal tapes might offer growth possibilities for their clients. Gerald Rafferty is a writer, counselor, and communications consultant. His interest in subliminal tapes developed from his fascination in studying not only how people communicate with each other but, just as importantly, how they communicate with themselves.

A primary goal in our practices has always been to educate our clients to provide them with all the effective tools available to help them develop solutions for the challenges in their lives.

In this book, references to clients in therapeutic settings are from actual case files from the practices of Lee and Joyce.

The promises of subliminal tapes were loud and clear: Lose weight. Quit smoking. End insomnia. Manage stress. Increase self-confidence. A host of wonderful achievements, all attainable simply by listening to a cassette tape. Who wouldn't get excited?

Excess weight, smoking, stress, insomnia, and lack of self-confidence are all symptoms of other, underlying problems faced by our clients every day. The promise of being able to relieve some of these symptoms so our clients could relax enough to delve into the underlying issues was exciting indeed. We investigated every possibility that showed some reasonable evidence of supporting our primary work as psychotherapists. We studied and applied hypnosis. We investigated and recommended nutritional programs. We taught meditation and visualization techniques. And we studied subliminal tapes.

Unfortunately, few of the subliminal products on the market lived up to their stated expectations. Many didn't work at all. Some seemed to work, but only in a hit-and-miss fashion. And these few successes could easily be attributed to the placebo effect, where the client's belief in the promised outcome of a tape or medication is enough to bring it about.

But we kept our minds open to the possibilities. We realized that the principles of subliminal tapes were basically and scientifically sound. Simply put, these principles are that our behavior is largely controlled by the subconscious; our subconscious minds hold our basic beliefs and attitudes; these beliefs and attitudes were formed from information we accepted from outside of ourselves; and if we could get our subconscious minds to accept new information that would change our basic beliefs, our behavior would then change.

We felt that the reason subliminals didn't work very well was simply because no one had yet developed an effective method for getting the new information into the subconscious mind. So we kept experimenting with new tapes as they came along. Imagine our surprise and delight when we started seeing more of our clients reacting positively to a new set of high-tech subliminal tapes.

Suddenly these new tapes seemed to be working, and not just with our clients. Stories of subliminal successes were popping up in the psychology journals and in the mass media. And all the successes were not from the same brand of tapes. There seemed to be a huge leap forward in the effectiveness of subliminals.

More and more companies were manufacturing subliminals, each company with its own special secrets and claims of phenomenal success. Subliminals began appearing on racks in bookstores. Subliminals were being advertised on television, and television time is very expensive. Clearly there was a growing interest in subliminals.

What was causing this? Why now? We got curious. We began asking questions.

Was there something new about the technology of manufacturing subliminals? Was it the new kind of music used for the masking sounds? Was it the scripts? Was there a breakthrough in understanding the grammar and syntax of the subconscious mind? Was the public simply ready for subliminals in a way that it had not been and therefore, greeting them with less suspicion and more openness? Was it just marketing? Was it a combination of all these things and still other things we hadn't thought of?

We embarked on a research program.

The general press provided stories of reported successes or failures of subliminals. The general theme of these stories depended greatly on the viewpoint and research done by the writer. At the time there were only a couple of books available about subliminals, and they focused mainly on the use and abuse of subliminal techniques in the advertising industry. The thrust of these books is that we, the consuming public, are under constant subliminal siege by the unconscionable masters of manipulation in the advertising industry to buy every kind of product from whiskey to crackers, that the subliminal appeal is almost exclusively through sex (with a little fear of death thrown in for spice), and that all of this is being supported by unethical manufacturers who couldn't care less about how you are manipulated to buy their products, so long as you buy them.

These books raised as many questions as they seemed to answer. Our investigative questions to reputable executives in the advertising profession left us unconvinced about the books' claims. The people we spoke to had no knowledge of sexy subliminal encouragements being inserted into national advertising programs. Indeed, the amount of conspiracy needed to keep such a widespread activity hush-hush is almost unimaginable.

But beyond this we were interested in the positive applications of subliminals — how they might be used as support tools in a therapeutic setting.

We turned our attention to the academic press and were rewarded with an explosion of published work on the research and experiments going on with subliminals. College campuses proved to be laboratories for subliminal experiments, with an unending supply of eager subjects.

Here again we found a wide variety of opinion. For every positive report about the success of subliminals we found a negative report about their failure. One team of researchers would conduct a thorough and very detailed experiment that proved, to their satisfaction, the effectiveness of subliminals. Other researchers would read the first report and write their own paper criticizing the conclusions, the methodology, and the scientific validity of the first program and conclude that subliminals did not work. Sometimes these criticizing teams would try to duplicate the original experiment, sometimes not.

An example of an attempt to duplicate one researcher's work took place at Xavier University. Two researchers there, Hovsepian and Quatman, duplicated one of the studies Wilson Key quoted to support the claims in his first book, *Subliminal Seduction*. Their findings, however, did not support the claims of the original study. "Key reported a study in which two intact college classes of 100 subjects each were shown a male model selected randomly from an advertisement in Playboy magazine. The subjects were to evaluate the model on a five-point scale of masculinity-femininity. [It seems there was some confusion whether the model was actually a male or a female dressed in male clothes.] The first class was shown the model's picture as it appeared in the advertisement. The second class received the same advertisement, but with a 1/3000th of a second presentation of the word *man* flashed every five seconds across the picture. The latter group rated the model significantly higher in masculinity."

The Xavier researchers' experiment went like this. They selected a full-faced picture of a model whose sexuality was not at all immediately apparent. (The model was a male.) They randomly divided their hundred students into four groups. Group I was simply shown the picture. Group II was shown the picture with white light flashing every five seconds (to suggest that they were getting a subliminal message). Group III was shown the picture with the word *masculine* flashed (for 1/1000th of a second) at five-second intervals. Group IV was shown the picture with the word *feminine* flashed at the same speed and intervals.

This experiment showed no difference among the groups in rating the model masculine or feminine. On the face of it we seem to have conflicting results. However, a closer look shows us that the experiments were not exactly alike.

In the first study we had two groups of 100 students each. One group was flashed the word *man* for 1/3000th of a second. In the second study the groups consisted of only 25 students each. They received different words — *masculine* and *feminine* — flashed for 1/1000th of a second.

These may not seem like big differences. But when we're dealing with the mind, even the slightest discrepancies can have a major impact on the reported results. We found these kinds of discrepancies many times in our research.

A study in Russia in 1983 showed conclusive evidence that measurable physiological changes occur as a result of subliminal stimulation. In this study two groups of men were wired up so their brain wave activity could be measured. One of the groups consisted of confirmed alcoholics. The word *vodka* was flashed subliminally to both groups. Only the alcoholics showed any change in brain activity, and this was measured and recorded by computers.

In a study done through the University of Northern Colorado, a group of 73 sixth-grade students were tested to see if subliminal stimulation could affect their attitudes and achievement in mathematics. The phrase "Math can be fun and easy" was embedded in background music for one group. The other group received only the background music. Results? No differences in either group's attitudes or achievement in math, and no differences between the male and female students.

As early as World War II, training techniques based on minimal perception were conducted at Ohio State University. Researchers flashed silhouettes of enemy aircraft on a screen for gunners to identify. At exposures of 1/100th of a second, where the images were clearly visible and consciously recognizable, U.S. Navy gunners were trained to identify more than 2,000 silhouettes at one sitting without a single mistake. Pilots of friendly aircraft were very interested in this study. The same principles and methods were later used to train football quarterbacks and student drivers.

In a study conducted through the University of Wisconsin, 43 seventh-grade students were tested to see if flashing subliminal messages on a computer screen, while a spelling improvement program was running, increased the students' spelling achievement. Messages such as "I'm OK," "I'm great," "I learn," and "I succeed" were flashed on the screen at subliminal speeds. The students were then tested for spelling achievement and academic self-concept. No improvements were noted in either area.

As is evident, most studies reported in the academic press involve exacting experiments with defined groups functioning within very controlled limits. There are exceptions to this. Every once in a while subliminals are tested with a broad spectrum of the population, with few if any of the academic controls.

For over six years an FM radio station in Montreal, Canada, ran a special subliminal program at 11:30 at night. The aim was to use subliminal messages to help reduce stress in the program's listeners. The method was to broadcast subliminal suggestions masked by the sound of pleasant, relaxing music. Each program opened with an explanation to listeners about what they were going to hear, as well as a series of simple pointers to help attain a relaxed state.

Initially the program was to run only a few months to test listener reaction. Six years later the program was still running with phenomenal success. The audience rose from 3,500 to 21,600; a recording made of one of the programs sold over 50,000 copies. In response to an audience questionnaire, 74 percent indicated relaxation or decreased tension, 22 percent a feeling of warmth, 20 percent a feeling of lightness, and 90 percent listed sleepiness.

And so the research continued, from positive to negative and back to positive again. Gathering accurate information about subliminals got to be a little like trying to nail Jell-O to a tree. Every time it seemed we had some valid information, some provable results, some good working theories, we'd come upon yet another report scientifically proving beyond doubt that what we had just accepted as truth was, alas, false.

What to do? What to do?

We concluded that anyone trying to investigate the new and exciting field of subliminals would find what we found and be, to say the very least, unsatisfied. As more and more of our clients got interested in subliminals, they approached us with more and more questions about them.

How do they work? Are they legal? What am I listening to? Could I be manipulated to do anything I didn't want to do? Are the changes permanent? Can I listen to them in the car? Can I listen to them while I sleep? Is there a difference between a $6.95 tape and a $69.95 tape? What's the difference? How do I know that?

Good questions. All of them. And as we searched the literature we found no ready answers. There were lots of claims from people who manufactured tapes and wanted to sell them, and many of those claims often conflicted with each other. There were reports of experiments with conflicting results. But there were no ready, dependable answers.

This was quite understandable. With all we think we know through all of our sciences, what we're finding out, really, is that we've only just barely scratched the surface of knowledge. And this applies to almost any field. The physicist's description of the world just a few hundred years ago was of a bumpity-bump, billiard-ball kind of world with hard, definable atoms banging and smacking into each other. This picture evolved to an image where everything was Relative to everything else. Then we saw the world as being composed of waves and energy flows. And now physicists think it's all tied together with something they're calling superstrings. We're still trying to get it right.

When we come to the study of the mind, we're like blindfolded seekers sitting in a pitch-black darkroom with our hands probing through two holes in an otherwise-sealed black box. Our hands are stuffed inside huge, pillowy boxing gloves and we're trying to grasp a tiny, flickering, bouncing, squirming pinpoint of light.

We do the best we can. We create theories of how we think human beings work. Then we watch people, and we listen very carefully, and we see if we're even close to some truth. We see that what we call truth seems to work for 30 or 50 or even 60 percent of the people, 50 percent of the time. And we use that as a building block to create yet another theory, and we watch and listen some more, and on it goes. We do the best we can.

When it comes to the study of subliminals, the whole procedure gets pretty tense. Now we're applying high technology to a string of theories that we think fairly accurately describes how the mind works. We think the mind is basically divided into two parts — the conscious and the subconscious. We think the subconscious mind forms and then stores our basic beliefs and attitudes about ourselves and the world we live in. We think those beliefs and attitudes act as our beacons, our probing lights, our gyroscopes by which we guide ourselves through life. We think the subconscious mind responds to the same words and grammar and syntax that our conscious minds use to communicate with each other.

Recent studies lead us to think that the subconscious mind can be addressed directly through the body by a series of sounds and beats and rhythms and pulses. And that the subconscious mind translates all these into thoughts and feelings and beliefs and attitudes that we can use to change our behavior and, consequently, our lives.

We saw a very real need for some information and some guidelines about subliminal tapes. We saw that this did not exist yet and decided to write our own book. We began our research by stating our list of questions. Our initial reading and hands-on work with clients formed a layer of information upon which we built certain theories. These theories led to yet more questions, which led to more reading and more client work. This built another layer of information. Then more questions. And so on.

What you have in this book are the results of our work so far.

What we've tried to present you with here is a guide to understanding and using subliminals, taking them, as much as possible, out of the realm of the dark and mysterious. We'll give you some history, lots of accounts of studies both here and abroad, and lots of cases of the successful use of subliminals. We'll talk about the studies that supposedly show that subliminals don't work. We'll discuss the physiology and psychology of subliminals, the technology, the legal issues, the messages, and the other parts of subliminal tapes. We'll talk about testing subliminals for personal use and about choosing and working with them.

We constantly refer to "one manufacturer" or "another manufacturer we interviewed" because what we're reporting are claims and hearsay, and we don't want to pass along claims and promotional projections as fact. We don't want this book to be a guide for competing claims: "ABC company has this in their tapes." "XYZ company has that in the their tapes." You see, when it comes to subliminals, it is a very difficult process to objectively analyze the product and determine if it really has this or that.

The purpose of this book is to give you enough information to help you evaluate the many claims of the tape manufacturers and to give you some tools to help you decide whether a particular tape is working for you or not. But this is just the beginning. Our work with subliminal tapes continues. In Appendix B we briefly introduce The Institute for Subliminal Studies. We established the institute to further our studies of subliminal learning; to perform actual test studies; to test particular tapes with a live audience; to monitor, support, and help coordinate academic and scientific investigations; and to issue evaluative reports.

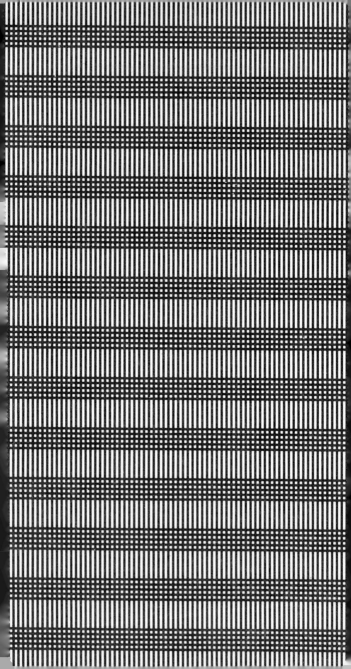

3
Technical Notes

Mary was a good student. She always liked school and got along well with her teachers. Her parents were very involved in everything that Mary did and carefully scrutinized every paper, every exam, and every report card. They were perfectionists and, despite their love for Mary, criticized everything that Mary did. Near the end of high school Mary became more and more fearful of taking tests and writing papers. Though she knew the material, her mind would frequently go blank. In her freshman year at the University, she began to draw complete blanks at every quiz and every test. The material, so clear in her mind the night before, disappeared when she reached the classroom. Her therapist had heard of subliminal tapes that were supposed to be helpful in test taking. Mary used them for one week prior to her midterm exams. She passed the tests, with room to spare. Here's the way Mary puts it: "I knew I knew the material, but I could never get it out before. These tapes help me to get what I know out of my head and down on the paper." The tapes didn't make Mary any smarter; they simply helped her perform better.

The story you've just read is true. Indeed, all the stories you'll read in this book are true accounts of people who have changed and are changing their lives by using subliminal tools.

We investigated the claims of the people we quote in this book. We worked with our own clients, using subliminal tapes. We've actually seen people who introduced subliminal tapes into their life-change programs lose weight, stop smoking, reduce their adverse reaction to stress, and effect other observable changes in their lives. Indeed, through extensive computer research we investigated the reports of thousands of experiments and tests involving subliminal stimulation.

Subliminal stimulation, both auditory and visual, has a quantifiable and noticeable impact on us. We're bombarded by subliminal stimulation all the time. All day long we see, hear, smell, and feel things that we're not consciously aware of, yet we react to them — and we react strongly. We immediately like some people we meet, yet dislike others. We feel comfortable walking into one strange room, yet uncomfortable and tense and suspicious in another. We're driving our car, daydreaming about one thing or another, when suddenly we swerve and avoid a serious accident. And it takes a few moments to realize we actually "saw" that other car before we were aware we saw it.

Recognizing that we do react to all sorts of undirected subliminal stimulation (stimulation we're not consciously aware of), it's not too great a leap in logic to consider creating specific subliminal stimulation that would generate specific, predictable reactions. That's the basic premise underlying subliminals. Would it be possible to create a tool that would get specific words and sounds to bypass conscious awareness and effect some change in a specific area of a person's life?

That's the question we set out to investigate, and we've come to a conclusion.

Subliminals work.

Having said that, we have to immediately backpedal and say that not all subliminals work. And of those that do work, some do not work as well as others. And of those that work better than others, not all of those will work equally well with every person.

It's a little like saying that food is nutritious, that food works for us. One immediately has to say that all food is not equally nutritious. In fact, some manufactured foods (what we all know and love as "junk foods") are so lacking in nutrition that they are without value and sometimes can even be harmful. Dr. Gershon M. Lesser, in his important book *Growing Younger: Nutritional Rejuvenation for People Over Forty*, devotes an entire fascinating chapter to the rejuvenation diet. In it he discusses food as fuel and offers some remarkable and practical information about the fuel value of various foods. He creates handy tables listing good foods and bad foods. Do you have any idea what actually went into your body at lunch all dressed up as a cheeseburger? You'll find out in Lesser's book.

In this book we'll discuss the whole idea behind subliminal tapes and how they impact us (a bit like discussing the basic idea behind prepared foods and how they work or don't work). We'll take this further and discuss the kind of subliminal products you're likely to encounter in the marketplace and how you can judge which ones will work for you. We'll give you criteria and tools to use in this judgment (much like giving you the means for evaluating which foods are likely to work for you and how you can find them and use them to your benefit).

Let's start with some definitions. In this book we often use the words *subliminal* and *subliminals* as nouns to refer to a particular audio or video tape product that offers you subliminal information or to a whole group of these tape products. We propose that subliminal tapes have already taken their place in the market as generic goods and that in the near future, if you haven't done so already, you'll walk into a multipurpose store or department store and ask a clerk, "Do you sell subliminals?" much the same way you now ask, "Do you sell books?"

Where did the word *subliminal* come from and what do people mean when they use it? The words *subliminal* and *subconscious* and *unconscious* are often used interchangeably, and when they are, people are referring to the subconscious or unconscious parts of our minds. More about our minds later. The word *subliminal* has two parts: *sub*, which means "below," and *liminal*, which means "threshold of awareness or consciousness." So, putting the words together, they mean "below the threshold of conscious awareness."

These thresholds are not fixed figures. For example, flashing images for 1/1000th of a second is the usual starting point for most experiments. Studies show that this is a workable visual threshold for most people, even though there are some people who can see things that flash a bit faster and some others for whom conscious awareness would end at a much slower speed.

When we come to audio thresh-olds we find a somewhat different system. Sounds are measured in decibels (db) — an arbitrary designation of the volume difference between one sound and another, just as an inch is a measure of length. All that means is that we can tell the difference between normal conversation, about 45 db, and whispering, about 25 db.

Look at the chart in Figure 1. You'll see a range of familiar sounds on the upper part of the chart with decibel amounts assigned to them. These are the sounds we receive into our conscious minds. The zero-decibel level is the cutoff where most people no longer consciously hear the sounds.

Scientists have found (through years of testing and study) that people are extremely receptive to sounds that occur below this threshold of conscious awareness. These sounds do vibrate in our eardrums and go to our minds. The difference is that they bypass our conscious minds and go directly to our subconscious minds. They are called subliminal sounds.

However, the sounds on the subliminal tapes you will purchase are above the threshold level. Most manufacturers record their scripts at around the eight- to fifteen-decibel level, and they record their masking sounds (usually music or rushing water) at around twenty-five to thirty decibels. So you are not getting messages that are at or below the subliminal level of sound awareness. You are getting messages that bypass the conscious awareness because they are below the level of whispering and they are masked by the music or water sounds.

If the masking sound was deleted and you turned the volume way up, you'd probably hear the messages. You may or not understand the messages, because some manufacturers record them at very high speeds to get the maximum number of messages on a single tape.

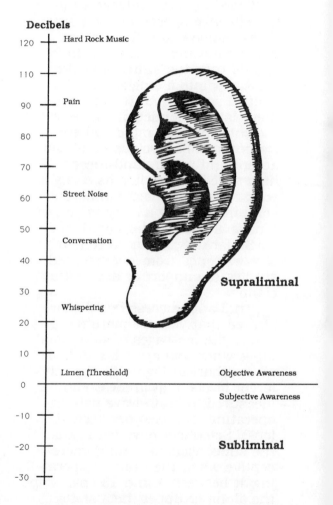

Figure 1. Range of Human Hearing in Decibels

There's some controversy over the effective speeds of the messages. Some researchers claim that time compression and high speeds turn the string of spoken messages into a single, high-pitched squeal. And this squeal, they claim, is undecipherable by the subconscious mind. Others claim the subconscious mind can accept and understand these high-speed strings just as easily as your conscious mind can accept someone reading a story to you in a normal voice and speed.

So far we've seen no conclusive evidence from documented studies to support or deny either claim.

Trial and success has demonstrated that you are more receptive to the messages of subliminal tapes when you are relaxed. Look at the chart in Figure 2. The different levels of awareness can be measured in brain wave patterns operating in cycles per second (cps). Scientists have found that the subconscious mind is more receptive when the brain is operating at between 7 and 13 cps, or in the alpha or upper theta states.

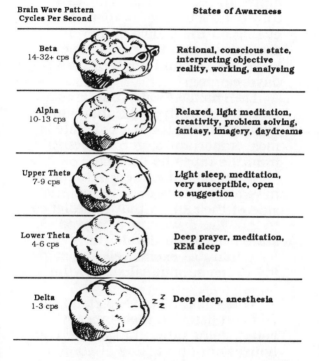

Figure 2. Human Brain Activity and States of Awareness

Throughout the day, as we go about our activities, we move pretty easily between the beta and alpha states. One moment we're fully conscious and aware and focusing on the people and events around us, and the next moment we're relaxed and imagining and daydreaming.

Dr. Thomas Budzynski, a noted researcher in the field of subliminals, says that the relaxed state is most important to get full benefits from the tapes he designs.

Some manufacturers actually have a conscious message on one side of their tapes that is designed to talk you down into a relaxed state before you devote thirty or forty minutes exclusively to listening to the subliminal side of the tape.

Other manufacturers claim that you can listen to their tapes while you're doing other things, such as housework or working at your desk or watching television. And they say that their tapes are specially designed, using unique sounds and messages, to get you into the alpha (the more receptive) state.

Napoleon Hill, in his world famous book *Think and Grow Rich*, tells us that in his opinion the subconscious mind responds best to ideas that are introduced to it wrapped in the wonderful warmth of positive emotions. He goes on to list what he considers to be the seven major positive emotions: desire, faith, love, sex, enthusiasm, romance, and hope.

It's our experience that people accomplish the most in a growth program when they have their thoughts and emotions integrated, working in the same direction. Indeed, if the opposite occurs — if you're deep in the throws of negative emotions while trying to think positive thoughts — you'll experience conflict and stress and no positive growth at all. So we would recommend a bit of all three of these suggested modes. Be relaxed. Generate some good, positive emotion such as enthusiasm or desire or love. And perform some tasks around the home or office while you listen to your tapes.

A general word of caution here: Because some tapes induce relaxation, it is never a good idea to listen to subliminal tapes while you are operating any kind of machinery, such as driving your car.

Most tapes can be played on any tape player; however, a good stereo system is recommended for tapes that are made for stereo. If possible, try listening to the tapes with earphones. They give you the full effect of the stereo by blocking out all other sounds. Many manufacturers take into account the fact that the left and right sides of our brains respond differently to certain sounds and, indeed, even to certain verbal messages. They produce their tapes to take advantage of this by having certain sounds and messages come predominantly into the right ear and others into the left. If you play them on a monaural tape player, you may not get the full benefits that the manufacturer intended.

It's important to see if a tape is designed to take advantage of stereo. Some tapes are not.

Some programs are available on compact disks. These special disks have revolutionized the recording and playing of music because they are totally free of audible interference, mechanical noise, or distortion. It seems reasonable that these qualities would enhance the effect of subliminal tapes also. But there's some controversy. To make compact disks the sounds must be digitized by a computer, i.e., transformed into a numerical format a computer can process. The regular tapes that you buy don't do this.

There's some debate over whether or not digitizing the human voice portions of subliminal tapes reduces their effectiveness. Here again, the industry is still too young to prove or disprove the claims one way or the other.

While we're talking about voice, it's also important to remember that tapes are made using a male or female voice. This could have some impact on you. Which voice would be more appropriate for you? Some tapes are made in male and female versions, the only difference being whether the messages were recorded using a male or female voice. Sometimes the contents of the messages are edited to be more feminine or masculine. Because of early childhood trauma, some people might be highly resistant to either the male or female voice. This would be something to discuss with your therapist.

One manufacturer told us that he initially records the messages read by a woman. Then he androgynizes the voice — uses a computer to move the voice somewhere between male and female tones. (You've probably heard this "computer" voice on TV shows or computer demonstrations.) Evidently he hopes this makes the messages on his tapes more universally receptive.

The improved technology available for making subliminal tapes is one of the reasons why tapes have had a sudden burst of acceptance and popularity. We fully expect technological advances to constantly improve the effectiveness of subliminals. Indeed, we receive almost daily news about some innovation or other that offers new promise for new achievements. That's another reason we established the Institute for Subliminal Studies. We want to have a constant monitor on the technological advances in this fascinating industry and to provide a means to share the information with others. We talk more about the Institute for Subliminal Studies in Appendix B.

4
Psychology of Subliminals

Carrol had decided to go back to school in her mid-thirties. In order to enter the program she was interested in, it was necessary to pass the Graduate Record Exam (GRE). After working with the study materials for a few weeks, Carrol began taking the practice tests at home. Her scores were dismal — 40 to 50 percent was the most she could manage. It was suggested to her that she experiment with a subliminal tape dealing with concentration and ability to pass exams. In one day, her scores on practice tests increased from 80 to 90 percent, and two weeks later she passed the actual GRE with flying colors.

Teresa, who also returned to school after a break of a few years, says this about her tape experience: "Within a few weeks [of listening to "Joy of Learning" and "Winning at Exams" tapes], my at-

titude toward school had changed considerably. I was better able to study and concentrate. My first grade after listening to the tapes was an A."

At any given point in our lives we are the total of all the thoughts, feelings, and experiences we've had so far. We quite literally *are* those things. We could be nothing else. Our actions are the outward manifestation of our beliefs, thoughts, and feelings. Our feelings are our own instant physical response based on our estimate or evaluation of outside stimuli, based on the deepest beliefs we hold about ourselves.

You could not be thinking, day and night, about becoming a prize-winning journalist, yet suddenly and miraculously wake one day to find that you have instead become a supersuccessful business manager, running a dynamic, pulsing company, doubling its product line every year and tripling its profits. Life just doesn't work that way.

Biographies demonstrate a very simple idea. Essentially biographies string together the actions of a person's life, presenting us with a sum total of who they were and what they did, hopefully in an interesting, storylike way. Excellent biographies, such as *Einstein: The Life and Times,* by Ronald Clark, or *The Passion of Ayn Rand,* by Barbara Branden, take us by the hand on a secret voyage into the subject's thoughts and deepest beliefs. Barbara Branden did such a thorough and convincing job of presenting the reader with Ayn Rand's thoughts about herself and the world around her that at the book's end the reader is struck by the clear inevitabililty that of course Ayn Rand became the famous novelist that she did — she could have become nothing else.

The simple idea demonstrated by biographies (and your own life) is that we are what we think; we become what we think about. Of course, we are more than just our thoughts. We are thinking, feeling, behaving beings. All three areas are intertwined, with each area powerfully affecting the other.

There's a formula used by psychologists that states $E + R = O$.

That stands for Experience + Response = Outcome. Experiences are the many things that happen to us in life. Outcomes are the resulting actions we take (our behaviors) depending on our Responses to those Experiences. And the way we respond to life's experiences is a direct result of our deepest beliefs and attitudes about ourselves and the world around us.

$$E + R = O$$

Experience　Response　Outcome

Figure 3

Think about yourself and any small group of people and what happens when it rains. Some people respond to rain in a very easy and accepting way. They see rain as a perfectly natural phenomenon, make some minor adjustments in clothing and schedule, and move on with the day. Sometimes they'll even get giddy and playfully use the rain as an excuse to do some different, silly activity. "Let's get a pizza delivered and cuddle up and watch an old movie."

Other people see rain as a curse and imprecation for humankind. It's wet. It's cold. It makes driving difficult. It messes your clothes. It hides the sun. It makes a day gray and dour and bleak. "And, no! I won't be able to get that done today! Don't you see it's raining!"

Same experience. Different people. Different responses. Different outcomes.

Both people's outcomes were the result of their responses to an experience. Their actions were a result of their thoughts and their thoughts were the result of their basic beliefs and attitudes. And most of our attitudes and beliefs were formed many years ago in childhood and reside in our subconscious mind.

We don't want to leave the wrong impression here, so let's digress for a moment. There's another adage in psychology that goes like this: There are always two people who come in for therapy, both residing in the same body — the person who wants to change and the person who doesn't. And that's only two for one. Some folks walk around with an entire, very active, very vocal committee in their heads. We're complex creatures. We're multifaceted. We're not straight-line, predictable, Pavlovian beings who'll always salivate when the bell rings. Sometimes we'll hear the bell and say, "No thanks. Not now. I'm full. I have a headache. Try me in an hour." Sometimes we're moved by the mood of the moment. And that mood is our response to yet another experience that may be deep and powerful and sets the tone for the day. The same person might respond to rain differently on different days. And that's perfectly natural. In fact, it could be stressful for us if we tried to force ourselves to always react the very same way to every experience. Our broad discussion here, as pertains to the use of subliminals, has to do with the basic attitudes and beliefs we hold and not with day-by-day fluctuations of mood or temporary frames of mind.

Most of the information we used to form our basic beliefs came from other people, usually from our parents or those who raised us. This information came both verbally and nonverbally. We took this information in, almost completely unchallenged (we had no cognitive tools with which to challenge it), and it greatly formed our basic opinion of who we were, how we would see the world, and how we would evaluate the world and respond to it.

Not only do we take these inappropriate messages in but we spend a lifetime reinforcing them to ourselves. We get comfortable with who we think we basically are. More than comfortable, sometimes we're proud of it, even though we know on some level that it's not good for us. "That's just the way I am," we say, "Take me or leave me. You may do things differently than I do, but this is the way I do them and this is how I like it. This is me."

Picture this as an example. A little boy is constantly told that he will never amount to anything. That he is stupid. That all his efforts will always end in failure. That he is just like his father or uncle or whomever, who everybody knows is a bum. And all this verbal abuse is constantly reinforced by criticism and even laughter at every small attempt at achievement. This boy will not achieve success. This boy will not achieve joy in accomplishment. This boy will experience failure, because his basic belief system will have been set for failure.

Sometimes the information comes in nonverbally. Picture a little girl who was given something sweet to eat every time she experienced some discomfort. When she had a challenging day at school or experienced some small failure, Mom gave her something good and sweet to eat — to take the pain away. Whenever there was some accomplishment or cause for celebration, she was given something good and sweet to eat — to reinforce the good feelings. This girl will grow into a woman who turns to food (and usually sweet, empty, calorie-filled food) to boost her energy and self-esteem and to avoid feelings of sadness, depression, or failure. She will almost certainly have a weight problem.

These examples are so common they are almost cliches. And in that lies a deep sadness. They are so common.

These basic belief systems — the little boy's, which leads him to think he's a failure, and the little girl's, which leads her to think she must eat to feel good about herself — reside in the subconscious, the part of the mind that we don't tap into consciously every day. The man doesn't consciously and clearly say, "I'm going to fail at this regardless of what I do." The woman doesn't consciously and clearly say, "I feel bad. I think I'll eat a chocolate cream pie." They just sort of know that's what's going to happen, and they're not very surprised at all when it does. In fact they're very likely to say, "You see. That's what always happens. I don't know why. What's the use?"

When we have these deep-seated thoughts in our subconscious minds, there's only so much the conscious mind can do to combat them. For a few days, even a few months, our woman friend could probably stay on a diet. But it would be a struggle, a push, a fight all the way. She would never have the feeling that she was living the way she ought to be living. She'd constantly have the feeling that she was fighting herself.

Our man friend could throw himself into an activity — a new job, a new opportunity — again for a few months. But always there'd be this feeling that he was fighting himself. He could puff himself up with those catchy phrases they recommend in self-help books and tapes. "I can do it. I can do it. I will succeed. I will succeed." But he would always have the feeling of not-rightness, as if he were walking around in a suit and pair of shoes that were two sizes too small.

Both the man and the woman in our examples experience incredible feelings of stress. And this often leads them to other unhealthy activities or substances to reduce the stress, such as drugs and alcohol. They constantly feel like they are fighting themselves. And of course in a very real way they are.

The theory behind subliminal tapes is that we can reeducate ourselves, we can replace these old beliefs and attitudes by appealing directly to the subconscious mind with new verbal messages. The claim is that the subconscious mind can directly receive and understand these new verbal messages. And if something is good and it works, the usual next thought is that more is better. So we have some tapes that supposedly contain millions of messages to replace the millions of old negative messages.

And we can see that in some cases this really does work. The many studies and experiments cited in this book are evidence of that. We can be and are affected by information that we receive below the conscious level. In other chapters of this book we discuss what constitutes an effective or ineffective subliminal message. We'd like to add here just a few words about how we recommend that you use subliminal tapes as a part of your psychological growth program.

These tapes are not an end-all product in themselves. It's clear that subliminals can and do have a positive effect on many people. It's also clear that most people need to play the tapes at frequent intervals, because their deep beliefs and attitudes seem to creep back into their lives and they start repeating old patterns. Perhaps this happens because people want the tapes to do all the work. A stop-smoking tape is only going to work for someone who really wants to stop smoking and is willing to put in lots of other effort, in addition to playing the tape. We know of a few cases where people listened to a stop-smoking tape, but they really didn't want to stop smoking. They listened to the tape out of a forced sense of cooperation or open-mindedness. The results were interesting. They got irritable, anxious, and cranky and within a few days stopped listening to the tape — and they continued to smoke. It seems evident that the tape's message was getting through all right, and it was meeting a deep resistance, a seeming need to continue to smoke. And this produced conflict. Most people try to avoid conflict. It's a natural response. But these people avoided the conflict by stopping their work with the tape, which might have resulted in some positive change. They chose to continue their smoking behavior.

The tapes can help with the motivation to change. They can stimulate and encourage, but they can't force you to do anything you don't want to do. And they can't effect a total change in you without your continued help and support.

A most important part of working successfully with subliminal tapes is selecting the right subject area to work with, and for this it's most likely that professional help would benefit you greatly. For example, one of the case studies we share with you in this book tells of a very effective use of a tape called "Abundant Energy." Lee and Joyce used the tape very successfully as an aid to get through a temporary situation. However, if you tried to use an "Abundant Energy" tape to combat symptoms of chronic fatigue, you could be making a serious error and putting yourself in danger of prolonged physical damage. Your fatigue may have a medical cause — a thyroid condition, a serious sugar imbalance, a nutritional deficiency. Before using a subliminal tape to adjust physical symptoms, you'd be well advised to consult your physician. Then again, your fatigue may be your body's way of reacting to a deep depression. If so, some work with your therapist is in order.

Here's another example. You find yourself being angry and short-tempered at work. You're suddenly reacting badly to the normal day-to-day stress of the job. You do a little self-diagnosis. You accept the job as a given. You decide that you're the one who needs to change, so you buy a couple of tapes on stress management and controlling a bad temper. You work with the tapes for a few weeks but notice no change at all. In fact, the situation is worsening. You return the tapes because you feel they didn't help you with your problem, and you decide to try your best to live with a bad situation. It may be that you were addressing the wrong problem. (You know what they say about doctors and lawyers who take themselves on as clients. Well, that works for laypeople, too.)

With some professional therapy or counseling, with a psychologist or career specialist, perhaps you would have seen that you were not the one who needed adjustment at all. It was the job that had gone wrong on you. Perhaps a recent acquisition brought in a new management team — this is a frequent and increasing cause of business stress. Perhaps you've outgrown a job you'd only intended to be temporary, five or ten years ago. Your heart wants to do what you really and truly want to do, and you feel confined, restricted and smothered. It would be a surprise if you were not feeling ill-tempered and stressed. With some guidance, you might have seen that a couple of tapes on self-confidence and self-assertion would have helped you to change your *relationship* to your work, rather than you trying to force yourself to change your *reaction* to it.

If you're bound and determined to go the self-help route, you can still get the help of professionals through their books and tape programs. Dr. Nathaniel Branden, the self-esteem psychologist and author of eleven books on self-esteem and romantic love, has all but perfected a sentence-completion technique in his practice and workshops. As used by Branden, this technique can quickly burst through layers of confusion, misdirection, and denial and help a client get right to the core issues that need attention. And often these issues are surprisingly different from what the client (and sometimes the therapist) originally thought they were.

Branden, in his audio program "The Psychology of High Self-Esteem," tells the story of a client who was having romantic fantasies about a neighbor. The client was experiencing considerable guilt and fear that the emotional bedrock of his marriage was in jeopardy. In therapy Branden worked the client through some sentence completions. Almost immediately it became clear that the client was experiencing serious difficulties at work — his creativity was stifled. He made some adjustments in his professional life and his personal life came right back in order. His sexual fantasies about his neighbor dissolved. Later, in fact, he laughingly and lovingly shared them with his wife. Branden talks about his sentence-completion work in just about every one of his books (see the Bibliography), but the book *he* refers readers to for a thorough description of the process is: *If You Could Hear What I Cannot Say.*

Let's look at an example of sentence completion. You're angry and frustrated, stressed out on the job. You try to convince yourself that you're stuck with the job and your only avenue of relief is to try to adjust yourself to a bad situation. But you read about sentence completion and decide to try it. You agree to courageously, spontaneously write out eight, ten, or twelve endings to a sentence stem. It goes something like this:

If I were to admit how much I really dislike this job—

I'd have to have the courage to tell someone.

I'd have to quit.

I'd have to risk doing what I really want to do.

I'd have to face my family's anger.

I'd have to face my family's fear.

I'd have to face my own fear.

I'd have to do something about my dreams.

Everyone would think I was a failure.

I'd have to try something new.

I'd have to change.

I'd be scared.

I'd be free.

You get the point. What at first seemed to be a stress-management problem was really a problem in confidence and the need for a career change.

If you're seeking a satisfactory solution, the process works best if you're working on the right problem in the first place. And we often need professional help with the diagnosis. Once you're sure you're working on the right problem, subliminal tapes can be an effective aid to solution.

One of the best things subliminal tapes can do is to help give you the experience of a feeling or action that you want. Once you have that experience, once you know that it can really be yours, it's up to you to put conscious effort into maintaining it. It's a lot like riding a bicycle or making love. You can't learn how by reading a book or talking about it. You simply have to do it in order to get the experience of doing it. And once you do it, once the experience is yours, it stays with you. You can pull it out of your memory bank whenever you need it. Let's go back to stress management as an example. You find yourself tense. You're overreacting or reacting badly to stressful situations. It doesn't seem possible to change or eliminate the situations, so you resolve to try to change the way you react to them.

You read a couple of books about stress management. You try counting to ten before you react to anything. You try meditation. You try deep-breathing exercises. These are all tried-and-true methods we can use to adjust our responses to experiences. And there are other very effective techniques. One of the coauthors, Lee, at one time had quite a negative response to the ringing of the telephone. He got stressed and tense. He considered the phone an interruption of what he was doing. That was on an emotional level. Rationally, he recognized the telephone as a perfectly legitimate, indeed a wonderful, connection point to the world outside. He didn't want the negative emotional response and decided to change it.

He made a list of all the good things that came to him through the telephone. New friends. New clients. New business. New information. Connections with family and loved ones. He visualized each of these, mixing the mental picture with powerful, positive emotions of love and excitement and desire and enthusiasm. He clearly saw all these new, wonderful happenings flowing to him like some great, gushing river coming right through the telephone wires every time it rang. He also visualized how, when he made a phone call, other people were there to receive it — eager and enthusiastic to give him whatever he needed. In not too long a time his emotional response to the ringing of the telephone changed. Now he has an entirely new behavior. When the phone rings he's interested, excited, curious, and optimistic and answers it with an endearing, uplifting enthusiasm his friends have come to know and love.

There are many exercises and activities in the therapeutic toolbag. And used singularly or in combination, they can effectively help us change our beliefs, attitudes, and behaviors. We consider that certain well-executed subliminal tapes can now be included in the therapeutic toolbag as adjuncts, as aids to a program of self-growth.

The promise of a stress-management subliminal is that within a day or so you'll react better to the stress around you. You'll somehow feel calmer, easier, right in the middle of a stressful situation that usually upsets you. Your mind will be clear. You'll see options you never saw before. You'll feel in control of the situation.

This actually happened with another one of the coauthors. Gerald had been working for a few days with a stress-management tape as part of our research and testing program for this book. Through a series of mishaps and forgotten keys he found himself forced to drive back and forth between two locations in Los Angeles during peak traffic time. The situation was most irritating and would have had the calmest of people at the boiling edge of anger and frustration. Sitting in the car in a traffic jam, he found himself consciously saying things like: "Don't waste your time being angry here. You're doing all you reasonably can. Yes, the situation is bad. But you're doing all you can. You're in control. Stay calm." He finished his errands calmly and with energy left over to do some creative work in the evening.

It sounds like these tapes are magic, doesn't it? It sounds like all you have to do is passively listen to a stress-management tape for a few days and you will never again overreact to stress. Your life will be changed forever. What's next on the self-improvement checklist? Sugar addiction? Smoking? Overweight? No problem. All you need do is pop a few tapes into the old sound system, and regardless what else you actually do, these problems will be resolved and eliminated. Even if you park yourself in front of the TV and become a coach potato au gratin, stuffing sweet, oily junk food into your mouth and sucking poison smoke into your pink, delicate, fragile lungs, the tapes will change your life, right? Wrong!

It would be a serious error for us to imply anything of the kind and a bigger mistake for you to conclude it, either from this book or from the claims of tape manufacturers.

This is a book about subliminal tapes, so we're necessarily isolating them from the many other growth tools available to you. If this were a book about football, we would talk pretty exclusively about football. We wouldn't constantly pull your focus out to the broad picture of athletics and remind you that athletic programs are good for you and how football fits into the overall scheme. Nor would we constantly compare football to baseball or soccer or tennis.

Since this is the chapter on the psychology of subliminals, however, a few words putting things into a broader perspective are in order. Let's return for few minutes to the application of a stress-management tape. Let's assume you bought and used one and it seems to be working.

A constructive course of action here would be to recognize that the tape helped you. It gave you the experience of handling a stressful situation from a place of power and control. You saw yourself in charge, acting instead of reacting. This is a perfect opportunity to get your conscious mind involved. Observe the difference in your actions. See how they helped you manage and deal with the problem instead of the problem managing you. See what you did and consciously resolve to repeat those actions. Do this until the new stress-management behavior is really yours, is really your new habit.

Without actions on your part, subliminal tapes will probably function only as emotional and attitudinal band-aids. You must deeply desire change in your life, and you must work hard to make the new attitudes and beliefs and actions solid and integrated parts of your life.

We have talked mostly about how changing your thinking, changing your scripts, can and will change your attitudes and behavior. But we don't want to leave you with the idea that this is the only path that the field of psychology has to offer to help you change your life. There are many paths, and a good psychologist will help you explore many of them.

Here's a little flow diagram that can help you think about the way we interact with ourselves and about some other ways we can effect changes. See Figure 4.

We can see ourselves as Thinking, Feeling, and Behaving beings. And these three activities are interrelated. If you change one, you

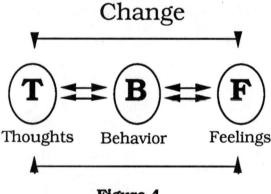

Figure 4

change the other. For instance, if we were to change our thinking, our feelings would change and our behavior would change. If we changed our feelings, our thinking and behavior would change. And if we changed our behavior, our thinking and feelings would change.

Think back to a time when you were feeling down and melancholy. You thought you'd probably spend the whole day that way. Suddenly you got a call from a friend telling you some wonderful and exciting news and inviting you to share it. These new, exciting thoughts changed your feelings. Your body seemed to perk up and you were ready to do something positive with the rest of the day.

You might have worked the same magic yourself, starting with behavior instead of thinking. Go back into melancholy for a moment. This time *you* change your behavior. You decide to go to the gym and swim or work out or get into a game of racquetball. Your body opens up with the exercise. Your feelings about yourself change. And your thoughts change. You actually find yourself thinking more positive, optimistic thoughts.

You get the idea. There are many ways to effect changes. Changing our thinking and beliefs and attitudes with subliminal tapes is one way.

△

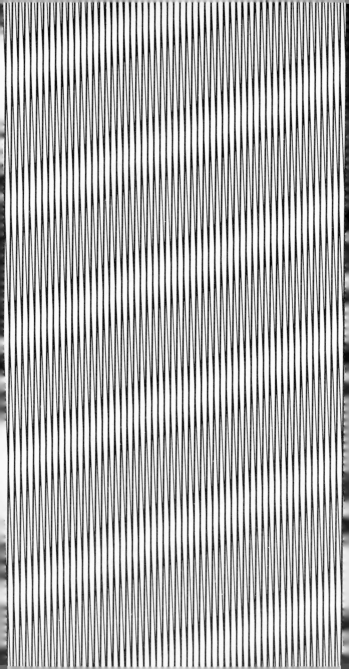

5
Temporary or Permanent

It was 10:30 at night and the five of us were still working. We were involved in the development of a business plan for a new venture. We were yawning, groggy — really running out of steam. And we had more work to do. Lee went to the tape player and put on a subliminal entitled "Abundant Energy." Without conscious awareness of the subtle effects of the messages on the tape, we continued working with increasing vigor until someone noticed it was 1:30 in the morning. We parted in high spirits, satisfied with the productivity of the meeting. Totally charged up, Joyce and Lee prepared for the night's sleep, but discovered that neither was very sleepy. The soft and gentle sounds of "Restful Night's Sleep," another subliminal tape they had been experimenting with, lulled them to sleep in less than twenty minutes. The others did not fare as well:

one continued working, another read, and one cleaned his apartment until 4 A.M.

> "Nothing is forever.
> Always is a lie.
> I can only love you,
> Till the day I die."

These simple, bittersweet words are from a love song from a movie called *The Glass Slipper*, which was a modern, musical version of the Cinderella story. The song presents an unusual sentiment in a field (the field of love songs) where the two most important temporal references are "last night" and "forever."

Permanence is the slippery, wiggling eel we all seek. Change, psychologists tell us, is the single most difficult process we human beings face. If we're going to put effort into something, by God, we want it to last forever, or as close to forever as a human being can get, which usually means a lifetime. For General Motors permanence is an annually renewable phenomenon.

We're offered permanence for

sale with embarrassing regularity. "How to create and maintain a permanent relationship." "Join our company for a permanent career." "Make this the last car [or house or TV or whatever] you'll ever buy." Even much of our clothing is permanently pressed.

It's no surprise that people look for permanent effects from subliminal tapes. But this doesn't seem to be any more realistic than seeking permanence in other areas of our lives. It's understandable, just not very realistic.

The permanence argument gets us into the areas of time and frequency and tape quality and, probably most important, the claims of each manufacturer. Those who make the tapes often directly claim, and certainly imply, that whatever changes you seek you'll get and that those changes will be yours — permanently. No one claims, "Let us change your eating habits — for a day." No. They say, "Let us change your eating habits." And you assume this will last.

Will your eating habits change after just one listening? "Oh no," the manufacturers say, "You should listen to the tape at least a couple of times a day for at least a few weeks to get any lasting or permanent change."

When pressed about how long the effects will last, one manufacturer admitted, "Well, it depends a lot on the person, of course, and how serious the problem was. And usually we find that people will go back and use their tapes every now and again as needed — sort of like getting a booster shot. And that's one of the great benefits of our tapes. You can go back and use them again and again, at no extra cost. With hypnosis or any other kind of change therapy, you'd have to repeat the work at an additional cost." It's just great when someone turns a challenge into a marketing opportunity! He must have just listened to his "Peak Sales Achievement" tape.

There was one study done with school children where some effort was made to measure how long the effects of a subliminal program lasted. The program had to do with basic attitudes toward scholastic achievement. Positive effects were measured after subliminal stimulation. After a few days without continued stimulation, the effects were still measurable but they were declining. Beyond that there was no more testing. Even with this study, measuring the length of time the effects lasted was not really a scheduled part of the program. It was almost an afterthought. The children had to be returned to their normal schedules.

And therein, of course, lies the problem. Experiments are designed with a certain focus. They begin. They achieve their mission or they don't. And they end. So far in our research, we've not seen a single study on the long-term effects of subliminals.

Informally, just watching the people with whom we've had close experience over the past year who were using subliminals, we've found that most people needed to go back to their tapes and play them again if they wanted some sense of permanence.

What we can look for, however, are very real changes in the areas where we seek changes. And these changes can be made permanent by a daily practice of reinforcement and recommitment. Let's look at smoking as an example.

Many people have used subliminal tapes to help them stop smoking cigarettes. Smoking is a very challenging habit to break. It combines behavioral, emotional, physical, and psychological patterns that run very deep and demand considerable effort to change. That's the bad news. The good news is that once the smoking has stopped, it will stay stopped — permanently — unless and until you decide to light up another cigarette.

This works in other areas as well. One subliminal tape we know of that produces great results in an area that is very objectively measurable is "Winning at Exams." Many students (some in their twenties in college, some in their forties taking real estate exams) report amazing results from working with this tape. In the past these students had great difficulty passing exams. They studied as hard as their classmates, sometimes much harder. They knew the material and could talk about it with great confidence in a non-test situation. But sit these same students in a room, hand them a printed test, and their minds went blank.

However, after working with a subliminal tape expressly created to overcome difficulties with tests, these same students were able to breeze through their exams. Mind you, the tapes didn't make the students smarter. The tapes helped them, as one student put it, "...to get the stuff out of my head and down on the paper."

These are somewhat objective and measurable areas. Either you passed the test or you didn't. Either you're smoking or you're not. With tapes that are designed to fight insomnia, either you're falling asleep or you're not. When it comes to areas where what you're working on is a basic attitude or approach, we find the lines between success and near success a bit fuzzy.

In areas such as stress management, feeling more lovable, self-confidence, goal setting, and the like, it gets a little harder to accurately judge effectiveness. And it's in these areas where people seem to slide back into old patterns more quickly. We are constantly undergoing stress and attacks on our self-confidence and finding the need to set more and more goals. We've found that even people who've achieved quick success in these areas using subliminals need to go back to the tapes every few weeks, because the effect does seem to wear off.

Weight control is an area that deserves special treatment. It is probably the most widely publicized use of subliminals. That's because there's such a painful consciousness in our country of weight as a cosmetic issue and what constitutes attractiveness. Consequently, there's a lot of money to be made from weight-control products. Also, weight control is one of the most deeply complex issues for us to deal with. It involves just about every area of psychology and self-image and self-esteem. And these issues can often require deep therapeutic work to achieve solid and permanent change. Because weight control is such a special subject, we devote a separate section of this book exclusively to issues of weight and how subliminals can effectively work in this area. See Appendix A.

6
The Power of the Mind

Jonathan didn't know whether or not he wanted to stop smoking. He wavered back and forth — yes I do, no I don't. Jonathan was in his fifties and had been smoking heavily for thirty years. He had made occasional unsuccessful attempts to stop smoking but had given the idea up as impossible. Encouraged to experiment with a stop-smoking subliminal tape, he reluctantly and skeptically agreed. The first report was that the tape was no good — it made him feel very angry. Several weeks later, it was noticed that he no longer had any interest in smoking and that he had casually given it up. He's not sure whether the tape contributed to his change in behavior, but it really doesn't matter, since smoking is no longer an issue in his life.

You are what you think about. A simple thought. And we repeat it throughout this book because it is such a deep underlying truth in our lives and has so many applications. This is not to say that every thought you think results in action. We don't act out all of our thoughts. Thank God!

The thoughts that you keep in your mind, however, can be and will be and are re-created in your body. There are many dramatic, documented examples of this in the annals of medicine.

Dr. Milton H. Erickson was a medical doctor whose pioneering work in hypnosis is a fountainhead in the fields of medicine, psychiatry, and psychology. One of the authors of this book, Lee, had the opportunity to study and work with Dr. Erickson some years ago. Lee was present at a remarkable demonstration during which Dr. Erickson let his students see, firsthand, the almost unbelievable powers of the mind. The incident was so remarkable and powerful that Lee remembers it vividly to this day.

"Milton gathered a small group of us in his office and said he wanted to give us a demonstration of hypnotic technique and the interaction of the mind and the body. He asked a patient with whom he'd been working (let's call him Jim) if he'd like to participate in a demonstration. Jim agreed and after a few moments we all settled down into an expectant silence. Milton told Jim that in a few moments he'd put him into an altered state but that while Jim was still fully conscious he wanted to describe what was going to happen. Milton then described the demonstration to Jim in detail. He told Jim that he would lightly touch Jim's hand with the burning end of a cigarette. He continued that Jim would most likely flinch and pull away slightly at the brief pain, but that the pain would not be unbearable. He also described to Jim the red blister that would appear on his hand, stay for a few minutes, and then disappear. All the while he was talking to Jim, Milton was smoking a cigarette.

"Milton then put Jim under hypnosis and asked if he was ready to proceed with the demonstration. Jim said yes and we all leaned forward a bit in our chairs. Milton then took an ordinary pencil and with the eraser tip lightly touched a spot on Jim's hand. Jim flinched and pulled his hand away. Milton assured Jim that everything was OK and in a soothing voice went on to describe again how the blister would appear and how there'd be a slight burning discomfort for a few minutes, but nothing that Jim couldn't handle.

"We watched, awestruck. An angry red blister was forming on the exact spot on Jim's hand where the pencil's eraser had touched it. Milton continued talking. He described how the blister would peak and then start to retract and, within a few moments, disappear. There was something that struck me then and stays with me still. It seemed that Milton was talking directly to Jim's body — right to the hand, right to the blister — rather than talking, as we usually do, to a person's head.

"Comfortable now in the midst of what moments before seemed like magic, we watched as the blister retreated and eventually disappeared. The entire demonstration took about ten minutes. Milton brought Jim back to full consciousness. Questioned by Milton, Jim reported no adverse or uncomfortable feelings. He remembered nothing of what went on. In fact, he didn't even rub his hand or show any evidence of the experience at all."

An important point about this demonstration is that it shows the power of the patient, not the hypnotherapist. Here's what Doctor Erickson and Ernest Rossi, coauthors of *Experiencing Hypnosis: Therapeutic Approaches to Altered States*, say about this. "It is now recognized that the most significant person in the hypnotherapeutic interaction is the patient, not the therapist. The patient's potentials and proclivities account for most of the variance (what actually happens) in hypnotherapy, not the purported 'powers' of the hypnotist. The therapist does not command the patient; rather, (as Dr. Erickson says) 'It is always a matter of offering them [patients] the opportunity of responding to an idea.' "

This was one demonstration with one patient.

There was a study done with a group of patients in England who had stomach cancer. While two-thirds of the group received two different forms of chemotherapy, one-third of the group received a simple, benign saline solution. We're all familiar with the expected reactions to chemotherapy, namely, nausea, vomiting, and alopecia (loss of hair); and these patients were no exception. All of them were fully aware of the possible consequences of the chemotherapy, but the possible benefits — remission of the cancer — far outweighed their fears and they volunteered for the program. Many of the patients receiving the two different kinds of chemotherapy did, indeed, experience the expected side effects in varying degrees. It's interesting to note here that while the percentages of nausea, vomiting, and hair loss were high, they were by no means universal. Not every patient experienced these side effects.

What absolutely astounded the medical researchers were the reactions of the patients in the group that received no chemicals at all. Almost 35 percent (34.6%) experienced nausea. Over 21 percent (21.5%) experienced vomiting. And almost 31 percent (30.8%) actually started to lose their hair. This is an unbelievable physical reaction generated completely by what the patients *thought* would happen to them.

Like Jim in the pencil experiment, these patients actually produced physical phenomenon based not on a physical cause but purely on what they thought would happen to them.

From the body producing adverse effects simply by thinking about them we come to the strange and wonderful medical reports of the body producing positive healing effects — straight from the mind.

Norman Cousins, in his thought-provoking book *Human Options*, gives us this powerful idea: "Nothing is more wondrous about the fifteen billion neurons in the human brain than their ability to convert thoughts, hopes, ideas, and attitudes into chemical substances. Everything begins, therefore, with belief. What we believe is the most powerful option of all."

Mr. Cousins clearly practices what he preaches. His famous book *Anatomy of an Illness* is the heroic account of his successful battle against a serious collagen illness (a disease of the connective tissue that is usually progressive and incurable) in which he used his mind, his belief system, to drive the life-threatening disease from his body.

It's a recent discovery that our brains actually produce pain-killing opiates that are even more powerful than the drugs we extract from plants or manufacture in our chemical laboratories. In *Anatomy of an Illness* Mr. Cousins reports on a study done with a group of patients who had just had surgery. The patients were given injections of morphine alternately with injections of neutral solutions called *placebos*, which we'll discuss shortly. "The placebo was 77 percent as effective as morphine. ... [and] the more severe the pain, the more effective the placebo."

This means that patients actually experienced pain relief even though they did not get an outside injection of a pain-killer.

We worded that last sentence very carefully. True, the patients did not receive a drug from outside of their bodies. True, the patients experienced relief of pain. So, it was the patients' imaginations that relieved them of the pain, right? Wrong. The brain (a functioning gland of the body, not a miracle spongy computer as it's often referred to) actually produces its own opiates, which in turn reduce pain. For these patients, pain relief was an inside job.

There is much talk about the placebo effect of subliminal tapes. What people are suggesting here is that it's the listener's *belief* that the tape will cause some change that actually causes the change. And from all the evidence we have from the medical profession, this is probably true, or at least partly true, in many instances.

A placebo is a "medication" that contains no active drug properties. Medical journals are filled with reports that placebos seem to be responsible for just as much healing and just as many adverse side effects as "real medicine." People respond to what they believe the effects of a placebo will be, both positive and negative. Their bodies actually produce physical symptoms, of health or illness, depending on what they believe will happen.

We've cited a few examples here. If you'd like to read about more examples and case studies in this area, we recommend Norman Cousins' excellent book *Anatomy of an Illness*. Mr. Cousins devotes an entire chapter to the placebo effect. He gives additional examples in his book *Head First: The Biology of Hope*.

We have tested many people using what we knew to be a placebo tape — a tape with nothing on it except a masking sound of rushing water. Our experience was that the placebo tape didn't seem to have much positive effect at all. When using a full subliminal tape, however, these same people tested positively. But we don't offer this as scientific evidence. It was all rather informal. To our knowledge no official experiments have been conducted to test the placebo theory with subliminals.

There is ample evidence that your belief system is one of the most powerful tools you can bring to any of your efforts designed to change your life. Your desire for change and your belief that you can change are the best gifts you can give yourself. In fact, those two ingredients may well be enough for you to effect any changes you want in your life. The rest of the tools you use are simply helpful aids.

Any program you develop for personal growth and health should include medical and psychological professionals. We're adding to that by saying that if you want change in your life, you'd best get the greatest ally you have working in your corner — yourself. Bring to your quest your deepest desires and wishes for self-improvement and your deepest beliefs that improvement is possible, and success can be yours.

7
Subliminal Scripts

Sally stopped smoking for the tenth time in the last year. It seemed that Sally could stop, but she couldn't stay stopped. Something would always get her started again. Eight months ago, she resolved to stop smoking forever. Her husband couldn't stand the smell in her hair, on her hands, in her clothes, or in the house. He was repulsed and she was desperate. So Sally stopped smoking again. This time, however, she has made it a practice to play a stop-smoking subliminal tape in her bedroom every morning while getting ready to start the day. The urge is gone, her compulsivity is gone. This time, she feels her smoking has stopped forever. She feels in control, and her marriage has shown remarkable improvement.

"In the beginning was the word ... and the word was made flesh." We get this from one of the holy men who contributed to the New Testament. He was probably referring to the idea that God became flesh by being born as a man on earth to bring salvation to his people. But there's another way to look at those words.

In a very fundamental way those words express a deep truth, a truth we're very familiar with in our new age because we hear so much about the powerful effect of positive affirmations.

The basic principle behind affirmations is that we are what we think; we become what we think about. Because much of our thinking is done in words, it becomes true then that we actually are the result of the words we allow to pass through our minds. "In the beginning was the word." We first think of the words or the words are suggested to us from our parents and others around us who influence us. "And the word was made flesh." Those words are our thoughts, and those thoughts become our actions, and the sum total of those actions becomes who we are.

This basic idea underlies the theory of subliminal learning, as well as many of the therapeutic theories in psychology. The idea is this. You are today the sum total of all the thoughts, ideas, beliefs, and attitudes that you have, from whatever source and for whatever reason, accepted about yourself.

Every day you are acting out the script of the person you deeply believe you are, and you are constantly becoming the person you think you are meant to be, supposed to be. You are being who you believe you are.

By the time we're adults many of us are unhappy about certain aspects of our behavior. We took up smoking, trying to fit into some teenage image of what we saw as cool and sophisticated, and now we'd like to stop. Our eating and exercise habits now result in weight gain, and we'd like to reverse that. Our reaction to stress and pressure leaves us depleted and angry, and we'd like to change that so that we resolve situations with command and confidence and calm. Perhaps our personal relationships are not all they could be because we protect ourselves from expected hurt; we won't allow the vulnerability that true intimacy requires. We act this way because in our childhood we either decided or we were told (by words and example) that we had to for self-defense. But in adulthood we find that those very same defenses are now keeping us from experiencing the full joys of intimacy, and we'd like to change that.

It seems one of the most effective ways to accomplish changes in who we are is to repeat the process by which we got to be who we are in the first place. And that is to begin with words, new words this time; to bring those new words into us until they turn into our thoughts; and to give those thoughts nourishment and encouragement until they turn into the actions that we want.

You see, we continue living out the negative scripts we have because we continue feeding those scripts with what psychologists call negative self-talk. Simply put, this translates into "We can't do certain things because we continue to tell ourselves that we can't do them." We become a self-fulfilling prophecy. Henry Ford is acknowledged for this little bit of wisdom: "If you say you can't or you say you can, you're right." And about this Mr. Ford was right.

You'll hear athletes say "It's 90 percent mental." What they mean is that if they can picture themselves doing something and they repeatedly tell themselves they can do it, chances are great that they'll do it. We become what we think, and we think what we picture and say to ourselves. And this has very immediate impact. We will do the very last thing we think about.

There's a baseball story that goes something like this. It's a critical game. Not the World Series, but a critical game nonetheless. It's the top of the ninth inning. The bases are loaded. The team at bat is behind by one run and their home-run slugger steps up to the plate. The pitcher's coach calls a timeout and walks out to the mound to give the pitcher a last-minute pep talk. He chats the kid up a bit. Tells him a joke about hot dogs and stale beer and retired umpires. Gets him nice and relaxed. Gives him one of those little affectionate pats on the butt. Turns to go. Stops. Turns back and says, "And for God's sake, whatever you do, don't pitch to this guy low and outside."

Now that you're familiar with the basic principles behind thought and action, you know how the story turns out. The very last thought in the young pitcher's mind is "pitch to this guy low and outside" (we'll talk a bit later about what happened to "don't"). We know that thoughts turn into actions. He gives the batter a beautiful pitch — low and outside. The slugger connects. Sends the ball out of the park. All four runs come in. The game is over.

Our well-meaning coach is beside himself. "How could he possibly throw the very pitch I told him not to throw?" How many anguished parents have said the very same thing, with different words for *throw* and *pitch*? Don't fall. Don't eat that. Don't be late. Don't forget. Only to find the opposite occurs. Little did the coach or the parents realize they were dealing with a law of human nature as powerful as the law of gravity. Drop an apple from the branch of a tree and it will fall to the ground. It will not hover in the air and test out a new theory of aerodynamics. It will not travel sideways over to the next tree and attach itself in the hope of joining a new, more progressive community of apples. It will simply fall to the ground.

And we will become what we think about; we will act out the running verbal script we play for ourselves.

While we still have the taste and picture of apples, let's recall another old saying using that mythic fruit. "The apple doesn't fall far from the tree." The usual meaning of this is that we tend to be like those who bore and raised us. This works in the biological sense. We are, and can only be, a unique combination of chromosomes and genes we got from our parents. This also works emotionally, psychologically, and intellectually. We got most of who we are in these three important areas from our parents and those who raised us. It's from these people that we heard the most about ourselves and the world we live in. And the things we heard became our beliefs, and our beliefs became our continuing self-talk tape and our actions.

Unfortunately, much of the talk we got from our parents and elders was negative, and that resulted in negative self-concepts and self-images.

It has been amply demonstrated that our actions can be and are affected by what we say to ourselves. We can create positive phrases and repeat these to ourselves to change our behavior. These are called affirmations. We affirm something about ourselves to ourselves until it becomes a part of ourselves. These affirmations are created consciously and repeated consciously. While this system works, it's sometimes pretty inefficient because it's trying to lay new beliefs over old, deeply entrenched ones. While we're trying to give ourselves new conscious affirmations our subconscious minds are repeating our old negative self-talk about the same subject, and the subconscious beliefs are much more powerful.

The new positive self-talk is called giving ourselves *affirmations*, and we call the old negative self-talk, the opposite of affirmations, *deformations*. We deform ourselves with our old negative self-talk.

The scripts of subliminal tapes are supposed to replace negative beliefs with new positive ones. And there are certain theories about what makes an effective subliminal affirmation.

Here are some of the best thoughts that we've been able to gather concerning the affirmations for a good subliminal script.

The affirmations should be positive. That seems too self-evident. Let's take a closer look at that. Psychologists tell us that it's best to avoid giving children instructions involving negatives, such as "Don't write on the wall!" or "Don't play in the street!" They suggest that we give positive alternatives rather than negative commandments: "Here's your very own pad for you to write on." "The back yard [or the park] is a good place to play."

Young children really don't understand negatives. A negative is a very sophisticated, rational concept that can only be understood by a trained, conscious mind. Think about it. To understand that a thing is *not* is pretty tricky and demands conscious concentration. For the most part, animals and small children understand what *is*; they don't really get what is *not*.

From all we know right now it seems your subconscious mind functions much the same way a child's mind does. It can only grasp positive information, presented in the here and now. A good subliminal tape avoids sentences with negatives, such as "Don't eat too much" or "I don't smoke anymore." If the subconscious ignores the word *don't*, the effect of the sentence would be reversed.

Much of the information we have about how we think the subconscious mind works we get from years of trial and success experimentation with hypnosis and neurolinguistic programming (NLP).

Good affirmations remain in the present tense. "I am relaxed." The subliminal mind understands *now*, not yesterday or tomorrow. Again, we see that this is much the way a child sees the world. Ever promise a child you'll do something next week, or take a long car trip with a child? Be prepared to hear a lot of "Are we there yet?" and "Is it next week yet?"

A phrase such as "I will relax" tells the subconscious mind that you are not presently relaxed. It's something that's going to happen later. It hasn't happened yet. And as far as the subconscious mind is concerned, later never comes. It's never tomorrow. It's always today. It's always now.

Good subliminal affirmations are short. Again, it seems the subliminal mind functions very simply. And lengthy, complex sentences only generate confusion. "I am losing from two to seven pounds consistently, per month, until I reach my perfect goal weight and will continue to visualize myself as I will look when all the extra weight is off."

Not only is this phrase too complex a grammatical structure for the subconscious mind, it has too many references to the future: "consistently, per month..." "until I reach..." "will continue to visualize..." "will look..." "when all the..."

Dr. Milton Erickson offered that it's best to address the subconscious mind from the three voices of English grammar. First person: I am. Second person: You are. And third person: He or she (plugging in the person's name) is. So a good three-pronged approach in hypnosis might be for you to say, "I am relaxed." For the therapist to say, "You are relaxed." And for both of you to talk about you as though you were a third person: "Alice is relaxed."

There's one more version that we get from NLP that goes, "It's OK to be relaxed." This last one gives an objective outside permission to being relaxed. "I'm relaxed and it's OK." "It's OK for you to be relaxed." "It's OK for Alice to be relaxed."

Of course it's difficult to use the third person, name-specific approach on subliminal tapes. A few companies are starting to offer personalized tapes, and those could include your name. Most of the good scripts we've seen use a combination of *I am* and *It's OK* statements.

Let's return for a moment to how we got our scripts originally. We received information in the second and third person. People said, "You are a bad child" or "David is a bad child" or "Alice is a bad child." We had to do the translating for ourselves. We looked around the room and saw that we were the only kid there. Certainly we were the only David or Alice in the room. "Ah ha!" we said to ourselves, "They must be talking about me. I am a bad child."

Just imagine if we had had a good, solid sense of ourselves and a firm grasp on our own self-esteem. We might have looked around the room and said, "Oh, that's just their opinion. That has nothing to do with me. If they had any vision at all, they'd see how wonderful and charming and brilliant I really am." There do seem to be some children who have the capacity to do just that. Most children, unfortunately, listen to all the negatives, internalize them, and make them a part of their belief systems.

So we're the ones who ended up saying, "I am a bad child." And that's why a good subliminal script would have affirmations such as "I am a good person now" and "It's OK to be a good person now."

No discussion of subliminal scripts would be complete without touching on what is referred to as the "oneness fantasy." Dr. Lloyd Silverman, a notable researcher in the field of subliminals for over twenty years, conducted a famous experiment using subliminal stimulation. He and Dr. Rose Bryant-Tuckett worked with sixty-four emotionally disturbed adolescents at a residential treatment school in Peekskill, New York. The students were divided into two groups. Both groups were seen five times a week for six weeks for exposure to subliminal stimulus using a tachistoscope. (A tachistoscope is a device that can flash slides before a viewer for periods as brief as 1/1000th of a second — much too brief for anyone to possibly consciously read what is on the slide; all a person sees is a flash of light.)

The first group of students would receive a subliminal stimulus — a statement on the flashing slide. The second group, usually called the control group, would receive a neutral statement on their slide. At the end of the six-week experiment the students were tested with the California Achievement Reading Test. The first group did "significantly better" than the control group. Also, the first group showed marked improvements in other areas as well: arithmetic achievement, self-concept, homework assignments, classroom participation, and self-imposed limits on TV viewing.

The subliminal message that generated all this improvement surprised, shocked, and stimulated the scientific community. Was it "I am learning better" or "I take tests easier" or "I am a better student"? None of these. The statement was simply "Mommy and I are one." The control group received the statement "People are walking."

"Mommy and I are one." Why would that phrase increase performance in any area? Psychologists have been arguing the point and testing it, with many variations, since this famous experiment. For example, Dr. Kenneth Parker conducted another six-week study with his students at Queens College in New York. The students this time were studying law. He divided sixty volunteer students into three groups. Group I, the control group, received a neutral message. Groups II and III received a subliminal activator. At the end of six weeks the students were given a law exam. Group I scored in the low B's. Group II in the high B's. And Group III in the low A's.

The message for Group I was "People are walking." The message for Group II was "The prof and I are one." The message for Group III was "Mommy and I are one."

The Mommy phrase has been tested in other languages. In 1982 Sima Ariam and Jerome Siller conducted an experiment on tenth-grade students in Israel. They translated "Mommy and I are one" into Hebrew and tested it against "My teacher and I are one" and "People are walking in the street." Are there no sidewalks in Israel? Of course there are. It's interesting, though, that the experimenters added "in the street" to make the Hebrew translation of "people are walking" a similar length to the phrase in English. That's how far some scientists will go in an attempt to replicate an experiment.

The results in Hebrew were the same as they were in English. The "Mommy" groups (there were two because of translation considerations) did much better on tests than the "teacher" or the "people" groups. The "teacher" group did a bit better than the "people" group.

The Mommy oneness fantasy gets a lot of attention and interpretation. Silverman spoke of it as a symbiotic merging with "the good mother of infancy." A sort of archetypal merging with the "oneness." But other scientists worked with "Daddy." They tested women with the phrase "Daddy and I are one." But that didn't get nearly the same results as

"Mommy". One experiment was done with male college students using a variation on the "Daddy" theme.

One group got the message "It's OK to beat Daddy." The other group got "It's not OK to beat Daddy." The two groups competed in a dart throwing contest and the "OK" group got higher scores than the "not OK" group.

Some tape manufactures use the "Mommy and I are one" phrase in the scripts of their tapes, regardless of what subject the subliminal is designed to work on.

It's clear that the scripts of subliminal tapes are important. And the arguments over the differences between scripts can be subtle indeed. Neurolinguistic programming would suggest that the phrase "OK to be relaxed" should work just great. Others would argue that full and explicit grammar is necessary and would insist on "It is OK to be relaxed" or "It's OK to be relaxed." The jury is still out on contractions.

There's also great controversy over the number of affirmations.

How many are best? Is more always better? There are two areas to the quantity question; one is grammatical, one is technological.

There are some tape manufacturers who claim to be able to pack over a million repetitions on a single tape. They do this by using multiple tracks (some use over 240 tracks), by speeding up the messages, and by using overlays and other technological secrets. There's controversy right here. Some say that if the messages are speeded up, time-compressed, and overlaid, the result is a high-pitched squeal that would be unintelligible to the subconscious mind.

Others claim that the subconscious mind can *hear* and understand messages recorded at great speeds, just as it can *see* messages flashed at great speeds. One manufacturer assures us that he can get great quantities of affirmations on a tape without using time compression. Only time and experimentation will prove what's best. No one yet knows.

The other issue regarding quantity has to do with the number of different affirmations on each tape. Some tapes are actually produced containing only five or six different affirmations, repeated over and over and over again. Other tapes contain 300 to 400 different phrases, all covering the same subject, repeated over and over. Which would be best?

The studies of linguistics and communication tell us that there are many proper forms of communication. For example, it seems that we can be divided into three broad communication groups: those who receive information best by *listening*, others who get it best by *seeing*, and still others who *feel* their information. The *listening* people would use and respond to expressions like "I hear what you're saying" and "It sounds right to me." The *seeing* people would use phrases like "I see what you mean" and "I get the picture." The *feeling* people would prefer "I grasp what you're saying" and "Yeah, I can get behind that." They really get their bodies involved.

Of course, none of us is all one way; we're each able to function on all three levels. However, studies have shown that most of us have a preference and respond more strongly to one of the three categories. For instance, you got through school OK, but if you were predominantly a visual person, you probably had more trouble in classes that were all lecture — no textbooks and no blackboard work or other visual aids.

Subliminals, of course, are all auditory. But beyond that, suppose the scripts of a particular tape were written using almost all feeling words, because the person writing the script was a feeling person. A visual person would be two steps removed from effective communication. The best scripts, then, would be written to appeal to the broadest possible audience, and this would require scripts that repeated the same or similar messages in words that would appeal to all three categories. This would clearly require more than five or six affirmations.

There's another reason why more affirmations would make a tape more effective for a broader audience. Take for example a tape designed to help people relax.

Suppose all the imagery on the tape had something to do with water — relaxing ocean waves, floating in a boat, etc. This would not appeal at all to people who don't like being around water; they might prefer mountain country or flat, quiet deserts. And that particular tape probably wouldn't work as well for them. It might not work at all. For some people walking is a wonderful exercise and would be a great suggestion on a weight-loss program for them, but it would completely miss the mark for others.

Incidentally, if you're interested in learning whether you're an auditory or a visual or a kinesthetic person, there are tests available to help you find out. You might check with a psychologist friend or call the psychology department of a local university.

Many manufacturers will include the scripts right with the tapes you buy. Others will supply them if you call and request them. And still others will not tell you what's on their tapes. They feel that their scripts are the major point of difference between them and their competitors, and they don't want to give their secrets away. They may feel justified in this; however, we feel you have a right to know what you're listening to.

We could not find any laws dealing with this issue specifically. However, we do have truth-in-packaging laws in the food industry now. Every packaged and processed food item you buy must contain a label stating all the ingredients that are in that package. It probably won't be long before someone will think to apply this law to subliminal tapes.

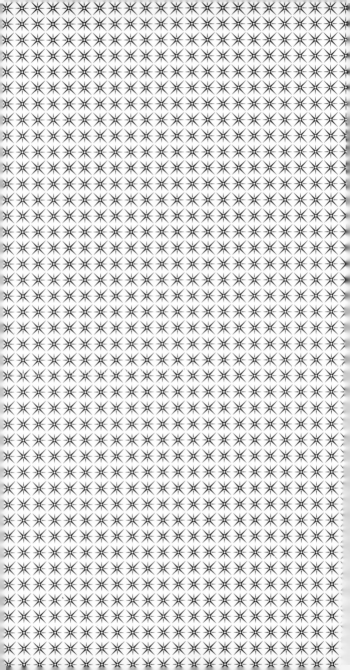

8

The Sounds of Subliminals

Weight control is one of the most difficult problems faced by a large portion of the population. The struggle with weight gain, the attempts at weight loss, and the subsequent weight gain are known to many, whose lives consist of this up-and-down yo-yo effect. Madilyn's life followed this pattern for thirty-two of her forty years. Her struggle began at age eight. She had already ballooned to 140 pounds and was three times the size of most of her classmates. Her life was a constant series of diets, weight-loss camps, spas, and doctors. Each one would result in her winning short-term battles. It wasn't until her basic, subconscious attitudes toward food and her body changed, with the consistent use of subliminal education, that she finally felt she had "won the war." The psychological drive to use food to fulfill many needs other than fueling the body is a strong and persistent one. When Madilyn's subconscious psychological attitudes changed, she was able to change her eating habits with consistency.

The first thing you notice when you play a subliminal tape is that you do hear something and that the something you hear doesn't sound anything at all like a voice telling you in words to change something about yourself.

Most likely you hear the sound of ocean waves rolling against and caressing the shore, the sweet rhythmic gurgling of a babbling brook with an occasional bird or frog announcing itself, or simply gentle music. Most tape manufacturers use one of these three.

Why were these sounds chosen over all the other possibilities? Why not loud thunderstorms or screeching rockets or the rhythmic rumbling of train wheels on tracks? Why not the slicing hush of the bow of a boat cutting through water, the technological hum of a generating station, the soothing sounds of a choir singing

Gregorian chants, or the murmur of a large group of people in busy conversation? (Did you ever wonder what all those people were saying in those crowd scenes in movies? It sounds like the director has them all milling about saying, "Rutabaga. Rutabaga. Rutabaga.") Some of these sounds would actually work very well.

The masking, or cover, sound used on subliminal tapes is chosen for its ability not only to cover up the sound of the messages but, just as importantly, to help you relax so that you'll be more receptive to the messages. The point is to get the messages to you without you hearing them directly. Or hearing them at all. One manufacturer received a lot of complaints because the music he selected had low points and spaces through which the message portion came through. Because his messages were speeded up (as many of the message tracks of these tapes are), listeners heard an annoying buzz in the musical gaps and returned the tapes.

Another manufacturer's tapes actually allow you to hear the messages if you turn the volume up and stand close to the speakers. The messages are there in real time, sounding much like a whisper.

The masking sound should be soothing and inviting to you because you'll be playing the tape over and over again. Another important criterion is that the sound be able to melt into the background so that you're not conscious of it. A drawback of tapes that use recognizable pieces of music is that the conscious mind hears the music and after a while may rebel at the repetition. That's why most of the music selected for subliminal tapes is a kind of floating music that doesn't seem to have the clear, identifiable sections that we expect in most good classical music.

One manufacturer we interviewed used the babbling brook sound rather than the ocean waves sound because the brook is a more constant and consistent sound. The sound of waves matches the actual flow of ocean waves and so rises and falls in intensity. Also, he claimed that the brook sound comes the closest to the sound the fetus hears in the warm safety of the womb. On the other hand, Dr. John Diamond claims that the rhythms of a Strauss waltz are the closest to the beats and pulses of the mother's heart that the fetus hears. Both views may contain some truth.

But the sounds do more than mask the messages. There are many studies being conducted on the impact of various sounds and rhythms on the human body. Dr. John Diamond is one of the pioneers in this exciting field, and he explains many of his findings and theories in his book *Your Body Doesn't Lie*. Dr. Diamond gives some amazing examples of how music affects the body. After reading his chapter "The Music in Your Life," you may never listen to hard rock again, and you'll have a tendency to keep a healthy distance from your TV set. Perhaps the most impressive piece of information in the chapter is a list of the names and ages of over one hundred long-lived musical conductors. It's an impressive list, with all the ages in the seventies and eighties. Good music seems to help keep people alive.

He also reports the results of a test that proves that our bodies receive music directly, not just through our ears. With the ears of some of his clients completely blocked, their bodies still responded to sounds. It was a fascinating experiment to read about. The application to subliminals is that whenever you're playing the tapes, not only are you getting the messages below your conscious awareness but your body is receiving directly whatever benefits there are from the masking sounds.

Along this line, Dr. Alexander Kirzhner has developed some techniques that are on the leading edge of subliminal technology. For many years Dr. Kirzhner, a dentist, studied the use of hypnosis as a tool to help his patients. From hypnosis he moved on to subliminal technology and found that he could help his patients just as well in less time. He began experimenting with sounds and developed a series of background sounds that seem to have a positive and beneficial effect on the mind and body. Kirzhner calls his group of special sounds and rhythms *substimulation* and includes them in the masking sound of a babbling brook on his tapes. He considers his substimulation so important to the effectiveness of his tapes that he's actually said that if he had to give up his scripts, he would, and his tapes would still have a beneficial effect. They wouldn't do all they could do with the scripts, but they'd still be effective.

Others in the marketplace think similar thoughts. The primary attribute of one set of tapes seems to be the musical sounds. Indeed, the literature describing these tapes states that "research has shown that specific sound patterns stimulate the optimal brain wave state for accomplishing a given task." These tapes offer selected sound patterns to help you increase your performance in a variety of areas: Concentration, Productivity, Creativity, Problem Solving, Action, and Reading/Study. These tapes were created based on the work of Georgi Lozanov, a

Bulgarian educator. Lozanov spent years studying the effects of different sounds and sound patterns on the learning process.

Almost as an afterthought, at the end of the advertising copy for this tape set, we find a few words about subliminal messages: "To enhance the program's power, subliminal messages have been layered below the music to augment the learning process and elevate your self-image."

There's other evidence that sounds alone can and do produce beneficial results. A few years ago a French doctor faced a very unusual challenge with a group of monks in a Benedictine monastery in France. Dr. Alfred A. Tomatis, an ear, nose, and throat specialist, was called into the monastery to examine seventy of the ninety resident monks, whose behavior had recently taken a bizarre turn. He found the monks listless and acting like "wet dishrags." They were sleeping late and working less, and they had started adding meat to their previously vegetarian diet. After careful medical examinations he found few physical problems that would cause the behavior. He dug deeper.

He found that the monastery had a relatively new abbot who, in an effort to modernize the centuries-old lifestyle, had, just a few months before, all but eliminated the traditional six to eight hours a day of Gregorian chanting from the monks' schedule. Tomatis knew of the benefits of sounds on the human body, especially the throat, head, and brain. He reasoned that the elimination of the chanting was a major cause of the problem and took immediate steps to correct it. He got chanting back into the schedule and went even further.

Tomatis supplied each monk with headphones and a cassette recorder programmed with baroque music with the lower frequencies filtered out. Within nine months all but two of the monks were back on the job, working, praying, eating their vegetarian diet, and full of their old energy.

"We are creatures of sound," Tomatis explains. "We live and breathe in it. And in giving these monks back their sounds — their own stimuli — we simply succeeded in reawakening them."

An increasing number of tape manufacturers are experimenting with innovative sounds for tapes. One company in New Hampshire produces a set of seven tapes, each of which generates a series of special tones that directly impact one of the body's seven chakras (major energy centers). These tapes are designed to clarify your perceptions and bring you into a state of harmony, emotional stability, and improved health.

So the masking sounds on subliminal tapes are just as important as the underlying scripts, and you should put thought into selecting tapes with sounds that are pleasing and appropriate for you. Of the three coauthors of this book, two of us, Lee and Gerald, like the babbling brook sound, mostly because it's the sound that most easily fades into the background until we're not even aware the tape is playing. We find that music, with its recognizable patterns, competes for our attention and awareness. The third coauthor, Joyce, doesn't like the babbling brook;

she finds the sound annoying and prefers the music tapes. Any annoyance will discourage continuing use of any therapeutic tool. We encourage you to investigate and experiment and trust your own reactions when choosing and using tapes.

While testing ourselves and our clients, we discovered another interesting facet regarding the sound of the tapes. The volume of the sound had an impact on whether a person tested positively or negatively to a tape. One person tested positively to a tape. We assumed that the combination of sounds and scripts was just right for her. However, when we tested the same tape on her again at a slightly higher volume she tested weak, or negative. Evidently you can have too much of good thing.

Pythagoras was an early Greek philosopher (582 B.C.) who founded a religious movement that studied the special relationship between numbers and music. He and his followers believed that the essence of all relationships could be expressed numerically. They were the first to establish the mathematical precision of music. And they used music for healing. One story tells of a vengeful, jilted lover who surrendered his angry feelings when a Pythagorean played a series of chords on a lute. Pythagoras himself was said to have "cured many ailments of the spirit, soul, and body" by playing music that he specifically arranged for each person and his or her particular ailments.

Isn't it wonderful how, in our zest and enthusiasm for our modern technologies, we sometimes learn things that, as a species, we already knew.

Testing Subliminals

Six women and two men attended a ten-week course on the "Anti-Diet Weight Control Program." During the discussions, a subliminal tape with messages that encouraged healthy eating habits and relaxation and the ability to control appetite played quietly in the background. The sound of bubbling water permeated the room and the underlying messages entered subconsciously. As the course progressed, members of the group began reporting changes in eating habits. Some reported these changes with surprise, and some with astonishment. In the sixth week of the course, almost all of the members of the group began requesting copies of the tape for themselves. A year later, good eating habits and maintenance of weight loss are still being reported by half of the original group.

There's an old saying that goes: "The proof of the pudding is in the eating." Like a lot of old sayings, this one has survived because it's true; it holds some wisdom for us.

Scientists can and have tested and scrutinized just about every conceivable activity or product, and they often arrive at conflicting opinions. This is certainly true of subliminals. If you have ten scientists, five in group A and five in group B, and they all perform the same or a similar test on a subliminal product, group A will say the product works and the proof is in the methodology and results of the test, while group B will say the product doesn't work and the proof is also in the methodology and results of the test.

There are many reasons for this and we really can't go into all of them in this book. (There are entire books devoted just to discussing the psychology and methodology of tests and the people who do them.) But there's another old saying that offers some truth here: "People will very often find exactly what they're looking for."

And those people will believe, sometimes to the death, their conclusions.

It wasn't too many years ago, just a few hundred, that almost all scientists agreed that the earth was flat and that it was the center of the universe. They really believed this and they'd kill anybody who said otherwise. From our perspective, sitting warm and cozy in the space age, we can smile at them and give them the proof-of-the-pudding argument: "We've been around the world and back again and you can believe it, fellows — it's really round. It fact, we've been to the moon and back again, and we've seen that the earth is not the center of the universe, far from it." Then again there are still people who believe the whole trip-to-the-moon show was all done with mirrors and cameras and stage sets. See what we mean? Get more than one person looking at something and you're likely to get more than one opinion about it.

Let's bring this closer to home. Look at the cigarette industry. Medical science has for years now been demonstrating the terrible effects of smoking on the human body: cancer, emphysema, blood diseases, and so on. Yet millions of people don't want to believe the evidence and still smoke. More tragic than this, millions of young people begin smoking every day. More tragic still are those people who put on the costumes of the scientists and smile into the news cameras and say that there's no evidence that smoking causes cancer or harms the body. Crazy, isn't it? Maybe not so crazy. These folks work for the tobacco industry and they're being paid to say such things; and they may actually believe what they're saying. It would be fascinating to study people's beliefs vis-a-vis the relationship of those beliefs to money.

So, different opinions abound on just about any subject you can think of, and this holds true of subliminals. Why wouldn't it? Subliminals as a subject for study are like any other. Scientists are still people, and they are lined up on both sides of the issue; even among those who agree that subliminals really do work, there are many different opinions about how they work, why they work, and what makes one work better than another. In this chapter we will tell you about many of the scientific experiments that have been performed to prove whether or not subliminals work. We conducted a thorough study of the field, and we'll share our findings with you so that you can see what's behind the different opinions and draw your own conclusions.

We've already shared our conclusions with you. We think some subliminal tapes work. And we base this conclusion on actual tests and research by others, our own work with clients, and by testing the audiotapes of many manufacturers on ourselves.

There are also many reports of field demonstrations involving real people supporting the conclusion that subliminals work. The most famous of these is the *Picnic* story. In 1957, at a drive-in movie theater in Fort Lee, New Jersey, an experiment was carried out that brought subliminals to national attention. The audience sat, relaxed and comfortable in their cars, emotionally involved in the romantic scenes between two top movie stars — Kim Novak and William Holden. Little did the audience members know that they were getting more than a good time at the movies. Flashing on the screen, right over the movie image, for 1/3000th of a second every five seconds (well below conscious awareness), were two messages: "Drink Coca-Cola" and "Eat popcorn." The experiment ran for a couple of weeks before it leaked to the news media and the results were tallied at the cash register. Coke sales rose 58 percent and popcorn sales went up 18 percent.

Public reaction — anger, fear, and suspicion — was swift, and rightly so. How dare anyone come sneaking into my mind when I'm relaxed and vulnerable and manipulate my thinking to their benefit! Had the last stronghold of personal privacy — our very thoughts — been invaded? Surely this outrage had to be stopped, and it was, immediately. There was much talk of laws and restrictions to protect the public. The Federal Communications Commission issued guidelines concerning subliminals in the public media. We discuss the legal issues surrounding subliminals in the next chapter of this book.

Outrageous as it was, the experiment did seem to prove a point — that our minds could receive information, projected to us below the level of conscious awareness, and we would respond to the information. Scientists had been experimenting with this idea in closed studies for some time, but here was a real-life example that seemed to prove the issue. It seemed to be a proof-of-the-pudding testimonial.

And that brings us to what we want to offer you here, your own personal test with which you can evaluate your own reaction to subliminal tapes. "Experts" are lining up on both sides of the issue of whether subliminals work or not. Many, though not all, of those saying that subliminals do work have a vested financial interest in convincing you — they manufacture and sell the tapes. Many of those saying subliminals don't work also have their own interests in mind. Perhaps they're trying to establish or protect their positions as academic and scientific sharpshooters, bubble busters, iconoclasts, devil's advocates. And some on both sides are just reporting quite honestly how they see the facts.

As we said before, people are apt to believe or disbelieve something for many reasons other than what the facts are. Politics is a perfect example of all this. Two opponents will square off for verbal combat over a single issue. Each will be armed with all the statistics and facts proving the case beyond a doubt for his or her side. Finally, at least in this wonderful country, when all the noise and confetti and truth and lies have settled and mixed with the dust on the floor, you get the opportunity to quietly and personally review it all and decide what's best for you.

You do that with everything in your life, whether you're choosing a doctor, a car, a place to live, or a romantic mate. You take the presenting information, pass it through whatever decision-making process you're comfortable with, arrive at a decision, and act on it. For some people this process involves squeezing their eyes very tightly shut and pointing their finger at a column of names in a telephone directory, or a place on a map, and going with whatever is at the end of their fingernail.

We're going to present you with some procedures that have a bit more structure than that.

Your Body Doesn't Lie

Here's a technique you can use in the privacy of your own home to determine whether any number of things are good and appropriate for you. There's nothing to buy. All the equipment you need you carry around with you every day. The procedure is called Applied Kinesiology; the equipment you need is your body and the cooperation of a friend. Applied kinesiology is a muscle-testing technique whereby your body responds in a dramatic and noticeable way to different stimuli.

We're all familiar with lie detectors and how they're used in cop shows to tell whether or not the bad guys are lying. Lie detectors are electronic devices that measure and record a person's pulse rate, perspiration, respiration rate, and blood pressure as the person responds to questions. The theory behind lie detectors is that your body reacts involuntarily when you are under stress, and that stress shows itself by changes in the four points being measured. When you tell an untruth your body automatically responds as though you were under stress.

As with most things in life, lie detectors don't work in the same way, every time, for everybody. And you can't always tell if a person is lying or not in answer to a particular question, because even a truthful answer may generate the symptoms of stress. For example, if a person were answering a question involving an old love affair or the death of someone close, the question itself could be stressful, regardless of the answer.

What is clear, though, is that the body gives off certain signals when it's under stress, and these signals can be observed and measured from the outside. Muscle testing, or applied kinesiology, is another procedure used to test whether the body is under stress. Developed in the 1960s by Dr. George Goodheart, applied kinesiology had immediate application in the field of nutrition. Dr. Goodheart found that he could use muscle testing to determine whether a patient was responding favorably or unfavorably to various foods. For example, a patient might test "strong" one moment and, after tasting some refined sugar, test "weak."

Here are the steps to perform a muscle test. Let's say you're going to do the testing with a girlfriend. You be the tester, and she's the subject.

1. Have your friend stand erect, right arm relaxed and hanging loosely at her side, left arm held out straight from the shoulder, parallel to the floor. It's best if she does not wear high heels; they make balance difficult. See Figure 5.

2. You stand facing the subject, placing your left hand on her right

shoulder for balance and your right hand on her extended left arm, just about at the wrist. See Figure 5.

3. Tell your friend that you're going to exert pressure downward on her left hand and that she should try to resist you as best she can by keeping her arm straight out. This is not a macho contest of strength. Nobody should be straining. That would only bring both of you to fatigue. You're only going to press down with about fifteen pounds of pressure. That's not much. You can get a sense of what that feels like by pushing down on any bathroom scale until you reach fifteen pounds on the dial.

You're ready to try a test. You push down. She resists. You'll find that her arm doesn't move. She's able to resist your pressure and her arm stays locked in a straight-out position. This is called testing *clear*.

4. Now ask your friend to say something that is obviously true, for example, "My name is [and she gives you her real name]." Apply pressure while she resists and you'll see that her arm does not move down. She is testing *strong*.

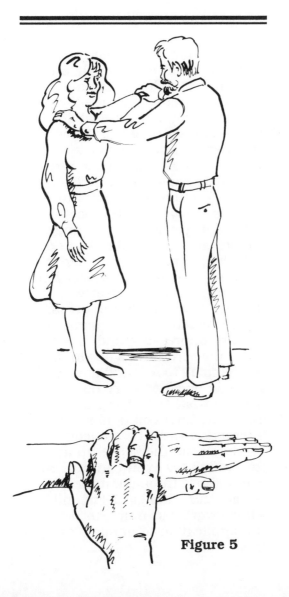

Figure 5

5. Now ask your friend to say something that is obviously untrue, for example, "My name is [and she gives you some other name]." Apply pressure while she resists and you'll see that this time her arm *does* move down. She is testing *weak*. See Figure 6.

This is the basic test. There are a few important points to remember. Always let the person know that you're going to apply the pressure just before you do it. The object here is not to try to surprise your friend and get her arm down. Say very clearly, "Resist." Then apply the pressure. Try always to exert the same amount of pressure and never make that pressure a strain. If you're going to ask and answer a series of questions, try not to anticipate what the answers are going to be. That could affect your interaction with the subject.

Here's another little tip about the testing that you can take with you and use throughout the day. We get this from Dr. Diamond, whose work did much to perfect the application of applied kinesiology.

Figure 6

Neither you nor the subject being tested should smile during the test. It seems the smile muscles are directly tied to the thymus gland, which controls the energy levels in your body. A smile can activate the thymus and increase your overall energy. A smile could erase the weakening effect of telling an untruth, and the arm might still test strong.

We've never seen smiling and giggling used as a method of beating the lie detector, but let's see if this doesn't pop up in the script of a TV cop show next fall. It seems we're constantly reminded of the basic truths of a lot of old sayings. You know the ones. "Let a smile be your umbrella." "Greet the world with a smile." "Smile and the world smiles with you." Smiling increases your energy. Remember how your grandmother or that funny aunt who always seemed to smell faintly of mothballs used to pinch your cheeks just under the eyes? Well, those are your smile muscles. And while Aunt Mothballs may not have known it, she was activating your thymus gland and thus increasing your overall body energy. You did have the good sense and motor power to get away from her as quickly as you could, right? See. It worked.

Applied kinesiology doesn't exactly test whether or not a person is telling a lie. It tests the immediate weakening of the muscles, the drop in body energy of a person undergoing some stress. And it can be used to test a wide variety of things.

Get yourself and your friend back into testing position. Test clear to be sure you're both ready and you have good resistance. Then have your friend put a little bit of refined sugar on her tongue. Test again. Almost without fail the arm will flop down with very little resistance. After she rinses her mouth out, try again. She'll probably test strong again.

Try a few other things. Have her think of a really unpleasant situation or person. She'll test weak. Have her think of something wonderful and loving. She'll test strong. Try the smile test. Try testing her while listening to blaring hard rock music. Weak. Right?

Now try something gentle and easy. You don't have to go too high-brow with this. Try one of those easy ballads by the Beatles. The test goes strong. Right?

There's much, much more to applied kinesiology than we've given you here. If you'd like to investigate it further, we give you some sources of information in the bibliography (see Callahan and Diamond).

We presented muscle testing because it's one of the tools you can use to determine if a particular subliminal tape is working for you or not, is a positive force for you or not. We've conducted these tests with a number of clients, using a number of different subliminal tapes. The results were startling and impressive.

Here's the procedure. Let's say you want to test the impact of a stress-management tape. This time your friend will do the testing and you'll be the subject.

1. Have your friend test you for clear to see that you're both connected and there's good resistance.

2. Concentrate on some situa-

tion or person that causes you a lot of stress. Test again. You will most likely test weak.

3. Play the tape for a few minutes. Just relax. Do what you would normally do while listening to a tape. Bring a stressful situation to mind, while still listening to the tape, and have your friend test you again. If you test strong this time, the tape is probably having a positive effect on you. If you test weak, the tape is probably having little positive effect on you, and it may actually be having a negative effect on you. We went into some of the reasons why this might happen when we discussed the importance of subliminal scripts in Chapter 7.

Subliminals and the Law

Are subliminal tapes legal? This is the first question many people ask about subliminal tapes. There seems to be some underlying sense that there's something about subliminals that should be illegal. We sense that we should be protected from being invaded by someone else's thoughts without our knowing it.

We have a deep sense of the right of privacy. And nowhere does this get more personal than with our very thoughts. There are many laws, at least in this country, protecting our physical privacy. These laws have their roots in the basic protection against unlawful search and seizure by our government. Our homes, our persons, even our cars and clothing are thus protected. This basic sense of privacy extends to the workplace. We all feel, almost instinctively, that our office or cubicle or desk or workspace is inviolate. We feel squeamish about going into a co-worker's desk to find that report. And we feel outraged if someone else does that to us.

We Americans have a right to our privacy and that's that. There have been legal challenges against junk mail, the idea being that our mailboxes are extensions of our private property. In a very real way they are windows to our privacy through which invaders can reach us with any message they want. "Why should I have to read material I didn't request?" we ask. So far, as we are all painfully aware, the courts have not decided to restrict junk mail. The fact that the postal service is a government-owned business and is largely supported by the companies that pay to have the junk mail delivered to us may or may not have anything to do with all this.

We feel invaded if we get telephone calls we don't want. The telephone is a very personal instrument, not to be misused or abused. Another example of the invasion of privacy is the fax machine — a kind of modern hybrid technological creation that's a cross between a telephone and a mailbox. The purpose of fax machines is to allow someone to send words and pictures to you over telephone lines and have the material reproduced on your desk instantaneously. Most businesses leave their fax machines on all the time. To not do so is a little like shutting off your telephone or putting a lock on your mailbox so that you cannot receive calls or mail.

Another open window to our privacy, and there are already people abusing and misusing it. Companies are sending out unsolicited advertisements over phones they've identified as being connected to fax machines. They're not only tying up your machine and phone line to send you something you may not even want — but they're even using up your paper.

In Arizona there's a law against leaving unsolicited flyers attached to the windshields of cars. It's an invasion of privacy. It's a source of litter. And it could be a driving hazard. Companies that do this, either because they're unaware of the law or choose to ignore it, risk a serious fine.

The whole area of technological invasion of our privacy, where government and business computers have access to every financial transaction we make (with the possible exception of cash buys at swap meets and garage sales), strikes fear in each of us.

But our minds are inviolate. Right? Our minds are the last sanctuary of ultimate privacy where no one can invade our thoughts with their thoughts without our permission. Right? Well . . . maybe.

There are reports of subliminal tapes being used in public places without the knowledge or consent of the people hearing the tapes.

There were two experiments run in a hospital in New Orleans. One was in a special treatment center where people came for injections. People often have emotional responses to getting punctured with needles, and fainting was a common reaction. Also, emotions ran high and volatile in the waiting rooms. A special subliminal tape with calming messages was played over the music system for a few weeks. Fainting was greatly reduced and the arguments and fights in the waiting rooms were almost eliminated. The subliminals were then stopped. The fainting and arguments increased almost immediately, as this special center always had an influx of new patients who hadn't heard the tapes.

At the same hospital another test was run in the doctors' lounge. A no-smoking subliminal tape was added to the music system, again for a period of weeks. No other changes were made in the use of the lounge. As determined by an actual count of cigarette butts in the ash trays, smoking was considerably reduced. Once again, after use of the tape had been stopped for a few weeks, smoking increased.

These tests caused great excitement in the community of subliminal researchers. And it's easy to understand why. The tests proved that subliminals worked. And because nobody knew they were listening to them, the placebo effect was all but eliminated.

But what of the right of privacy of the patients getting stuck in the special clinic, and the family members venting perfectly natural frustration in the waiting rooms, and the doctors and nurses who wanted to practice the secret principles of emotional alchemy by changing anxiety and fatigue into puffs of smoke? Hadn't they been invaded and successfully affected by someone else's thoughts?

Some other tests were run without the public's awareness. We talked about the experiment at the drive-in theater in New Jersey in 1957, but more subliminal tests have been conducted in public places without public awareness. And if the reports are accurate, some are going on today, even as you read this book.

Special subliminal tapes were played on the public address music systems of major department stores and supermarkets. The messages were plain, simple, and very direct. "Shoplifting is unlawful." "If I steal I go to jail." "I am honest." The results were impressive. Shoplifting was reduced considerably. And cash register shortages by employees decreased sharply — by an even greater percentage than the reduction in shoplifting. This last fact is understandable when you know a little about how subliminals work and consider that the employees listened to the tapes every day for periods varying from four to eight hours, while customers heard the tapes only while they were actually in the store shopping.

What do you think? Do you think the rights of the employees and customers of these stores were violated? The store management and the psychologists who created the tapes would argue that they were only encouraging people to do what they should be doing anyway. They were not trying to manipulate people into doing something against their will or something they shouldn't want to do; they were simply trying to protect their property.

And surely they should have a right to do that. Using subliminals in this way seems to be simply a different form of crime prevention. A different form of lock, if you will. A mental lock that works much like visible signs that state their message objectively: "Shoplifters will be prosecuted." "Trespassers will be prosecuted." A sign used annually in a pumpkin patch in San Jose, California, during Halloween season states very simply, very effectively: "Survivors will be prosecuted." When asked if the sign works, the owner smiles and says, "I haven't lost many pumpkins."

It's interesting to note that shoplifting and cash register pilfering were not totally eliminated. That may mean that subliminals don't work for everybody. It may also mean that those people who are hellbent on stealing are going to steal — no matter what. A policeman friend is fond of saying, "Locks keep honest people honest." And we must remember also that an act is not unlawful until there's a law that says you can't do it.

Opponents of subliminals would argue that it doesn't matter if the message or the intent is honorable or not. There are, always have been, and probably always will be many people who think that they should have the right to shape and manipulate the lives of others because they have access to some truth that largely escapes most of us. Opponents would also remind us, and quite rightly, that we as consumers must always be aware that a burning sense of self-righteousness can drive many people to bend integrity, if not the very law itself.

Surely it would not take much bending for some ambitious marketing manager of a department store to realize that if people could be *dissuaded* from stealing, perhaps they could *persuaded* to "use your credit cards and buy it today." (After all, the people were in the store already, and for heaven's sakes, they came in to buy something. Didn't they?) So, a quick wink at integrity, a phone call to an obliging subliminal manufacturer, a patch into the existing music system, and, presto, sales and profits are up. The manager gets a promotion and a raise and within two weeks buys the new car that's been beckoning from the showroom window, never giving it a moment of thought that the music system was playing overhead while the salesman asked the critical, closing question, "What color would you like the upholstery? Red or Black?" Ah, but life's a pretty little tune when you know what strings to pluck.

"There ought to be a law!" Right? Well, someday soon there probably will be. The more subliminals are used in society, the more opportunities there'll be for their misuse and the more probability of new laws to govern and restrict their use. Imagine signs in stores stating: "While you are on these premises you are being encouraged to buy something." "While you're in this store our music system is helping to keep you honest. You're welcome."

How about stores that played subliminals and didn't tell you about them? We could have a special task force of subliminal cops. Blending in with the rest of the shoppers in their civilian clothes, one would hardly take notice of the huge green parrots on their shoulders. These parrots would have the unique ability to hear through the music, decipher the hidden messages, and repeat them in a loud squawk. "Buy now! Pay later!" "Use your credit card." "You deserve the very best." Soon shoppers would be snapping their fingers and humming along as a parrot sang out, "Don't do the crime if you can't do the time. Doo wa, doo wa."

The Devil may have to take a back seat as the all-powerful instigator of temporary shopping madness. Laden with glittering booty, an embarrassed, indulgent consumer may someday soon say to a red-faced, angry spouse, "But honey, the music made me do it."

One gets giddy with the possibilities.

It's interesting to note that there are no laws yet governing or restricting the use of subliminals. There are some Federal Communications Commission (FCC) guidelines pertaining to the use of subliminals, audio and visual, over public airwaves. But these are guidelines and not laws. Following the New Jersey movie theater experiment with subliminals, laws were introduced in virtually every state. But as far as we could determine, not a single law ever got through the law-making process. One of the reasons for this is the same reason that many proposed laws get discussed but not enacted, while some others pass through very quickly. Special interest groups lobby for or against most proposed laws. And our lawmakers (human beings all) are greatly affected by the loud hounding and pounding of pressure groups.

But there's another reason and it's probably more substantial. Laws can only be effective if they refer precisely to this or that exact situation. And this can only be done using descriptive words and ideas. And sometimes, hard as we try, descriptive efforts at exactness escape us. It's sometimes like trying to put your finger on a little ball of mercury; every time you touch it, it squirts out in a different direction. This problem faces our lawmakers. Before a law can be passed about subliminals, our lawmakers need to be able to understand exactly what subliminals are and what they are not. No easy task.

Are billboards that flash by us as we whiz along a country road affecting us subliminally? What is the impact of having sweet-smelling perfume counters placed near the entrances of department stores? Should there be laws about such things? Should there be a law governing anything that we are likely to encounter and experience without being explicitly, consciously aware of? Because some subliminals are so effective and have such great potential, there probably will be laws concerning their use. In Appendix B of this book you'll find information about the Institute for Subliminal Studies, which is designed to keep current on this fascinating field.

One subliminal researcher, Wilson Bryan Key, sees the advertising industry as a hotbed of subliminal seduction. In fact, that's the title of one of his books: *Subliminal Seduction*.

One area where we may see laws very quickly pertains to the scripts. We have truth-in-packaging laws. These require manufacturers to list the ingredients of whatever food products they package. You didn't think companies went through the added expense of printing the ingredients on food labels because they were proud of all the sugar and chemicals they could list or because they felt you had a right to know what you were eating, did you? Some companies probably did list their ingredients before the laws were passed, because they were proud of the fact that their food contained only natural ingredients and they used the list as advertising.

You have a right to know what you're eating. And just as clearly, we think you have a right to know what you're listening to.

Some tape manufacturers already proudly publish their scripts and supply them along with the tapes. (In some cases, on close examination of the scripts, one wonders what they're so proud of. But we discuss that in the chapter on scripts.) Some manufacturers will send you the script separately, if you request it.

There's a common argument against publishing the scripts and it goes like this. The whole idea behind subliminals is to get around the ever-vigilant conscious mind and get the message directly to the subconscious mind (sort of like executing an end run around a tight defensive line in football). The point here is that if the conscious mind knew what you were trying to get into the subconscious mind, it would hold it up to close scrutiny, evaluate it, and if the message was found to go against other, long-held beliefs, the message would be overruled and discarded.

"Prosperity? Calmness? Self-confidence? Simple, loving joy? Not me. Not here!" your mental watchdog would say. "The only person living here is a poverty-stuck, frazzled, frightened, angry, sad individual. You must be meant for the people across the way there — that smiling couple I see taking peaceful walks in the evening, enjoying their neighbors. We don't need any of that positive thinking here. Go on, shoo! Shoo!"

This is a weak argument used mainly to protect scripts. True, we all experience a lot of mental chatter. And much of our self-talk *is* negative. And some of our basic beliefs are in direct conflict with each other. We discuss self-talk — where it came from, how powerful it is, and so on — in Chapter 4 of this book.

The argument that we can't afford to have our conscious minds know how we're trying to change ourselves goes against some very sound, ancient, and wise counsel we've gotten from spiritual leaders and people of great achievement. This counsel refers to positive, conscious affirmations you give yourself and/or whatever form of prayer you engage in. This argument also goes against the very conscious interactions you may have with a therapist.

You can change your actions and beliefs by telling yourself what new actions and beliefs you want for yourself. This works. It's a tried-and-true method for self-improvement, especially if you combine writing out the affirmations with saying them to yourself, over and over again.

A major drawback to using affirmations is that, depending on how deep or just how negative your basic beliefs are, it may take a very long time for you to change. And it may take a long time because your beliefs are warring with each other and you may give up the battle from exhaustion before the change occurs. It's true that subliminals bypass all this struggle and thereby can help you achieve change much quicker. But reading a script once to determine that it matches your goals and that it meets the criteria for a good script that you've gotten from this book will not sabotage your efforts to improve. The very act of deciding that you want to change some area of your life and then evaluating and using various help tools, such as books or tapes or therapy, is a very conscious process indeed. And while it may be fraught with fears and doubts, if you seriously want to change, you'll persevere and overcome.

One executive from a subliminal tape manufacturer gave an unusual and surprising answer when asked about the scripts for his tapes. He said, "So what if I did print the scripts? How would you know that that's exactly what was on the tape anyway? It's subliminal. You can't hear it. I could print anything on a slip of paper and put something else on the tape. How do you know you're getting what they say you're getting in vitamins? The point is, you don't. You just trust that you're getting what they tell you you're getting. Well, people just have to trust that what they're getting on my tapes is good for them."

I don't buy it. Do you? A response like that puts one a bit on guard, and it makes you wonder just what he does put on his tapes. He obviously didn't want to reveal the content of his scripts. He felt that his scripts were a major part of the quality of his tapes. They made his tapes better than other tapes. It's very hard work creating a good script. And he didn't want to give his competitors his hard work for nothing. Perfectly understandable. Yet there are other important elements that constitute a good, successful tape, and these differ from one manufacturer to another. We discuss these other elements in Chapter 8, "The

Sounds of Subliminals." This same problem is faced by food manufacturers, but they content themselves with the fact that while the ingredients are listed on the package, the varying percentages of these are not listed, nor is the method of preparation.

Here's something else disturbing about his argument. Of course people believe labels, and for good reason. People believe in the basic system of law; i.e., if you're required to tell me what's in something and you operate under the threat of some punishment for lying about it, you'll probably tell me what's in there. The disturbance goes deeper than this. We have a deep need to believe that what we tell each other about anything is true. Can you imagine what kind of a society we'd have if none of us believed anything we were told? We quite simply couldn't live under a system of deep suspicion.

Even without detailed ingredient listings, we expect labels to represent the contents of what we buy. When you want a can of peaches or pears, you naturally look for labels that say peaches or pears. You'd very quickly stop buying from a company that labeled something peaches which actually contained corn or yams or fish or whatever was left over in the plant. Any company would be very foolish indeed to try to lie about its products.

One baby-food manufacturer did lie about the contents of one of its products and incurred the full wrath and exposure of the consumer protection agencies. The company was bottling what it claimed was "pure apple juice," when in fact it was almost completely water and some sweetener, with very little apple content at all. The manufacturer was discovered, exposed and fined. The mechanisms of the free-market system in this country, especially with the high-speed methods of exchanging and publishing information, keep a basically honest and hard-working business community basically honest and hard working.

In order to properly evaluate a subliminal tape, it's best to know what's on it. You can use that information, along with the other tools presented to you in this book, to choose the tape that's just right for you.

11
The Future of Subliminals

We began this book by identifying subliminal tapes as one of the latest efforts, in a long line of efforts, designed to help us in our constant quest for self-knowledge, self-access, self-growth, self-change. We definitely see the subliminal tape as a new tool, a doorway, a passage, a new channel to personal power. It is a combination of some psychological principles and theories and technological achievement unattainable before the current age of computers.

We've shared with you our research and experience, from healthy skepticism to embracing enthusiasm. We've seen and felt mood and energy changes, feelings of personal power, both in ourselves and in others, as a direct result of using good subliminal tapes. We've not witnessed success in everybody who has tried a tape. Nor have we seen success in all areas within the same person. We've not seen perfection, but we have seen a difference.

The creation of subliminal tapes is an industry in its infancy. The industry is constantly struggling and experimenting and testing in its search for the perfect tape. The perfect affirmation. The perfect script. The perfect masking sound. The perfect medium — audiotape, videotape, TV screen, movie screen, computer screen.

We've tested products that are hardly more than low-decibel whispers of seven affirmations just barely masked by the pulsing sounds of ocean waves. Other tapes are the products of highly sophisticated electronic equipment and carefully authored scripts containing over 250 different affirmations. And now that we're on just about everybody's mailing list, we're constantly getting news of new research, new products, new theories, new efforts that are daily expanding the envelope of possibilities.

There's a product you can hook up to your TV to have affirmations scrolling across the bottom of the screen while you're watching your favorite programs. Of course, the messages are scrolling too fast for you to consciously see them; you are being subliminally stimulated. Another one hooks up to your computer so you can be subliminally stimulated while you work. Some products are only combinations of sounds — no scripts at all. The theory here is that the sounds are all that's necessary to stimulate certain organs in your body, which in turn stimulate certain chemical reactions in your body, which in turn stimulate certain thought processes, emotions, feelings, and attitudes.

What's in the future? What other ways might we devise to attain access to our deepest selves? We've heard talk of products that emit odors that would stimulate us subliminally and affect us much the same way as the tapes that are pure sound. How about approaching the mind directly through the skin? Almost half a century ago Dick Tracy wore his crime-stopper's, two-way wrist radio. Science fiction? Reports are that we'll see them on the market in the 1990s. In the movie *Our Man Flint*, James Colburn wore a wristwatch that, at a preset time, extended a prong that pulsed against his skin to silently wake him from a deep trance. We already have devices that people strap onto their bodies to fight chronic pain. They seem to be especially effective for people who suffer from chronic back pain. These devices work by pulsing the skin near the source of the pain with tiny electric shocks, which affect the nervous system in such a way as to lessen the intensity of the pain.

How far a reach would it be to create a device that would stimulate the skin in some way that would in turn stimulate the organs, or the brain directly, to produce chemical and emotional reactions in the body? Perhaps it wouldn't be a device at all. It could be a rub-on lotion that a friend or lover soothingly, lovingly works into your body.

Perhaps we'll soon have a combination of all these. Imagine a subliminal evening with your close one: listening to two subliminal tapes — one with scripts and a masking sound that disappears like white noise, the other an intricate arrangement of sounds to work on certain emotions; smelling the fragrance from a burning subliminal incense stick; in a room barely lighted with subliminal candles; laying on a soft cloth that looks like an electric blanket, but is wired not for heat but to give the body gentle electric impulses; lovingly massaging each other with subliminal lotion. Think of the subliminal impact of *that*. It makes a person want to stop writing and get to it.

Is this all too fanciful? What do you think? Not very long ago the concepts of the radio and the electric light bulb seemed so fanciful that their critics viewed their inventors — Marconi and Edison — as being on the soft edge of insanity. When Marconi's friends heard that he was seriously trying to create a device that would retrieve sounds plucked right from the air itself, without any wires, they actually tried to have him certified into an institution. Yet here we are today with radios that not only sit in one place and pick up one sound, they travel with us in our cars and strapped to our jogging suits, receiving a wide range of sounds. Edison's lightbulbs take us into the darkest crevices of the earth with tiny flashlights and light up the night sky proudly announcing the amazing achievement of skyscrapers.

The future of subliminals is alive today. Remember, we become what we think about. So tomorrow's realities are the featherlight thoughts tickling and stroking our minds right this moment. Tomorrow's subliminal products are already in the minds of the scientists and psychologists and electronic engineers who are creating this new industry. New ideas for subliminal applications will come from us — we who are writing this book and you who are reading it.

We invite your interaction and feedback. If you experiment with subliminal products, share your reactions with us, your successes and near misses both. Share your thoughts and ideas with us. If you have questions that we didn't address in this book, or didn't cover fully enough, write to us care of the publisher. Or contact us through the Institute for Subliminal Studies, which we created to continue our research into this fascinating field and to act as a clearinghouse for information, reports, experimentation, and speculation. (See a further description of the Institute for Subliminal Studies in Appendix B.)

We have enjoyed sharing this material with you. We've tried to present subliminals to you in perspective. We don't see them as some modern miracle of technological wizardry that by themselves can solve all your mental and emotional discomforts. We see them as working tools that, if created and used properly, can achieve substantial results as part of an overall growth program.

We hope we've given you some new information, some insights, some speculation, some fun, and, perhaps most importantly, some enthusiasm to relax with this new medium, experiment with it as a part of your program to achieve your goals — from success to joy in your relationships and personal peace.

△

Appendix A
Subliminals
for Weight Loss

The following material is extracted from a special booklet written by the authors of this book and designed to provide a focused explanation of how subliminal tools can be used in a weight-loss program. The people who read this section of the original booklet had already read many pages of material specifically written to introduce them to the whole concept of subliminal tapes. They had already purchased a weight-loss tape and received this booklet along with the tape. These sections stand alone as descriptions of the physiology and psychology of weight loss and were intended to provide more information while the person worked with the tape.

We decided to let this material stand as written. We're assuming, of course, that you're reading this appendix after you've read the text of this book, so you won't need constant reminders that this material is set in the context of using a subliminal tape for a weight-control program.

The Physiology of Weight Loss

You've heard it before and you're about to hear it again. "You are what you eat." More exactly, what you eat becomes who you are. Does moonlight become you, darling? So does a chocolate cream pie.

Think of your body as a highly efficient, constantly active chemical factory. Your body takes whatever you put into it — let's, for the moment, stick with all the stuff that loosely falls into the category of food — and breaks it down into its basic chemical elements. It absorbs the elements that it needs, stores the elements that it doesn't need right away but someday might, and eliminates the rest.

You are constantly becoming you

Your body transforms the elements it absorbs into the forms necessary to sustain, rejuvenate, and replace itself. It takes proteins and carbohydrates and minerals and vitamins and changes them into muscle tissue, bone fiber, organs, and blood. Estimates are that your body replaces itself — every single cell, and there are billions of cells — every seven years.

This process is going on all the time — every day, every hour, every minute, every second. All the food you eat is constantly being used up in your body's effort to sustain and replace itself. That's why you get hungry a few times a day. Your body needs more food.

Choose your model

This all sounds very simple and straightforward and efficient. And for the most part it is. We can compare the body to an automobile and the analogy will go a long way. How do you see yourself? As a tough Chevy truck, a slick Lincoln Continental, a solid Ford station wagon, a swift Porsche sports car, an undistinguished economy car, an overworked, battered taxi, or a playful Jeep? You pick the model that feels just right for you.

All the models are different, yet they all have fundamentally the same abilities and needs. With the proper hand and foot commands, they'll all go forward and backward, at different speeds. With the proper combination of fluids (fuel, oil, grease, water, antifreeze), they'll go forward and backward all day long — just like us.

We don't have to take this analogy to any extremes. It's very clear that if you put beer in your gas tank and Mama's chicken soup in your radiator, not only will you not get very far but you'll ruin a good machine. Just like our cars, our bodies need the proper kinds of fluids if we expect them to go forward and backward all day.

What are the proper foods?

A Zen monk once wrote a book about nutrition in which he suggests that the proper foods for a human to eat are those foods which naturally grow within a radius of a few hundred miles from where the person lives. This is a simple, unsurprising thought. We accept without challenge that

Eskimos would and should have a different diet than Arabs.

But few of us live off the land, or even near it, today. And with manufacturing plants mixing wide varieties of synthetics with natural foods and high-speed transportation systems bringing us exotic foods from faraway places, our choices are greatly multiplied and consequently confusing. To decide what is a proper diet, we need to get back to some basic ideas.

Proper foods mean proper nutrition

Proper foods are those we need for proper nutrition. And nutrition? That's the art and science of fueling the body for maximum health and efficient performance. Whenever we have an art and a science, people, being people, will separate themselves into two groups: those who are experts on the subject and those who follow the experts. And whenever we have experts we have different opinions.

And the differences are legion. "Eat eggs." "Don't eat eggs." "Drink milk." "Don't drink milk." "Eat wheat." "Don't eat wheat." There's no need to go on and on. What we can do is get underneath these differences by getting back to some fundamental ideas. All the experts agree that we need a basic supply of proteins, carbohydrates, and fats for optimal daily performance.

If we take in less than we need of certain items, and the body is not able to substitute or manufacture them from the other things we eat, we'll get sick. If we take in more than we need of certain items, and we don't use them by increasing our activity or eliminate them, they'll get stored in our body as excess fat. And it's always fat. The excess never gets turned into new fingers or teeth or kidneys. By the time you're an adult, you have just the right number of these body parts, in just the right size for you. You don't need extras, so you don't grow extras. The excess always goes to fat.

A word about calories

We talk about calories all the time. "The special calorie diet."

"Watch your calories." "How many calories are in that serving of chocolate mousse?" (As if it mattered, right?)

A calorie is a unit of measure, much like the inch for length and the decibel for sound. A calorie measures the energy, or heat-producing value, in food. We consume calories by eating food; we burn off calories by physical activity. From a given starting point, if you take in 2,000 calories within a twenty-four-hour period and use up 2,000 calories through physical activity, your weight will be back where you started.

The basic equation

If, however, you take in 5,000 calories of potential energy but only use up 2,000 through activity, you'll have 3,000 calories left over. And they will be stored in the body as fat, waiting to be used. That's the basic equation. If you add another 5,000 calories on top of the 3,000 you have left over, you'll have 8,000; and if you only use up another 2,000, you'll now have 6,000 potential calories waiting to be used. And so it goes to the point of overweight, which simply means more weight than we need.

Different foods carry with them different calories. A single serving of fresh spinach has about 20 calories; a similar serving of mashed potatoes has about 110; ground sirloin in a similar amount, 466. So we not only have to be aware of how much we eat, we also have to watch *what* we eat. Additionally, different foods have other kinds of important values for us — vitamins, minerals, etc. Further discussion of this is beyond the scope of this appendix. We recommend that you seek out some good books on nutrition.

How much is enough?

Someone once asked Abraham Lincoln how long his legs were (some folks have no social graces at all). His answer was wonderful, quick, and typically pointed: "They are long enough to reach the ground."

Lincoln's legs were long enough for him. They probably

would have been too long for Dolly Parton, and Dolly's wouldn't have fit Mr. Lincoln at all. We are each unique. A perfectly healthy weight for you will probably not be perfect for your neighbor. What is right for you at one age will not be right for you at another age.

On the average, it's perfectly healthy and appropriate for most women in their forties to weigh about fifteen pounds more than they did when they were eighteen. Our bodies change, our needs change, our activities change, and we need to be comfortable with the change. It's better to approach a weight-maintenance program with a goal that's appropriate and healthy for you, rather than getting fixed on some arbitrary number of pounds and creating anxiety to reach that number.

We recommend a visit with your doctor to discuss your new weight program.

The Psychology of Weight Loss

If our body sizes and weights were a simple matter of following some mechanistic formulas of eating only what we need, only when we need it, there wouldn't be millions of dollars spent each year on fad diets. More importantly, there wouldn't be millions of human hours sadly wasted in the agony of self-reproach by people who are unhappy with how they look and how they feel.

Why do we eat more of certain foods that result in weight gain?

It seems immediately clear that we eat for more reasons than to satisfy hunger or to keep up with our daily energy requirements. There are other issues involved than simple physiology. These issues are psychological. Our minds select and control what we do in all areas of our lives, and we select the kinds and quantities of foods we eat based on the beliefs and attitudes we hold about food.

If we wish to change the kinds and quantities of foods we eat, we need to change our basic beliefs and attitudes about food.

Let's for the moment put aside the basic drive of hunger as a reason why we eat. We all know that we eat because we're hungry; we also all know that we don't stop there. There are many other reasons why we eat, particularly why we eat certain kinds of foods in excess. What are they?

Psychologists have found that our relationship with food is deeply intimate, meaningful, critical, and powerful. It's right up there with sex. In fact, we'll see that many people use food as a replacement for sex.

Additional reasons why people eat

Here are some of the reasons, other than hunger, why people eat. Try saying these phrases out loud to yourself and pay attention to how you react when you say them. Some of these reasons will fit for you; they'll feel comfortable. You'll say, "Yes. I do that." Other reasons will not fit you at all.

Also, when reviewing the list, see if you can identify the common thread or common ground in all these reasons.

I eat to reward or entertain
myself.
I eat to reduce feelings of
stress.
I eat to avoid feelings of stress.
I eat when I'm feeling over-
whelmed.
I eat to get noticed.
I eat to gain authority.
I eat to celebrate.
I eat when I need love.
I eat because I'm afraid.
I eat because I'm alone.
I eat to console myself.
I eat to have something to do.
I eat to relax.
I eat to pick myself up.
I eat to feel secure.
I eat for companionship.

The list could go on, but this is surely enough to make the point: we use food to satisfy a lot of needs other than hunger, because we have a deep belief that food will satisfy these other needs.

To achieve maximum benefits with your weight-control program, consciously remember the reasons from the list that seem to fit for you. When you find yourself in those situations you can know that this is a dangerous moment for you. You are likely to overeat or eat the wrong foods. You can and should consciously decide to get yourself out of or somehow change the situation.

Have you discovered the common thread in that list? It has to do with where and when we developed the basic beliefs that food would satisfy all those other areas. Need a hint? Where and when do we develop almost all the other basic beliefs and attitudes that we use as guides throughout life?

Ah! I see the look on your face. You've got it. Of course, we develop those beliefs in childhood, usually with the help of some well-meaning adult.

When you did something you were supposed to do, one of the million "shoulds," you got a reward of a cookie or piece of candy. When you were teething and in pain, you got some good-tasting something to chew or suck on. When you were afraid or lonely or hurt, you were given something to eat to ease the pain.

As adults, when we get a job promotion, we celebrate with a good dinner. We join our peers to socialize over food. We bring candy to someone in the hospital or someone whose feelings are hurt.

The list goes on. In simple terms, we were and are taught to use food to *reward* ourselves for some of the accomplishments of life and to *relieve* ourselves from the unpleasantries of life.

The "S-word"

There was yet another common thread in the list of additional reasons why people eat. Did you see it? It has to do with the *kind* of food we were taught to use for reward and relief. It's not usual to bring a pound of carrots or green beans to someone you think needs a lift. Got it now? Sure. It's sugar. Sweets. The stuff that's pure calories, with almost no other food value at all. Excess sugar is not absorbed into your muscles and organs to do work; it's simply stored as fat.

Did you know that sugar used to be a prescribed substance in this country? It was prescribed to elevate moods and energy levels, which it does very nicely for a brief time. Then it drops the person even lower than they were before.

The psychological food cycle

Take a look at Figure 7. It shows how our basic attitudes and beliefs about food and our reasons for using food form continuous loops that are either positive or negative.

If we approach food from the positive and natural drive of hunger, we will seek foods that are good fuel for us — that provide energy, stamina, and strength. The results will be an appropriate body size, a good level of energy and physical activity, and a positive body image. We will use our bodies naturally and energetically, and that will lead to natural hunger and start the cycle all over.

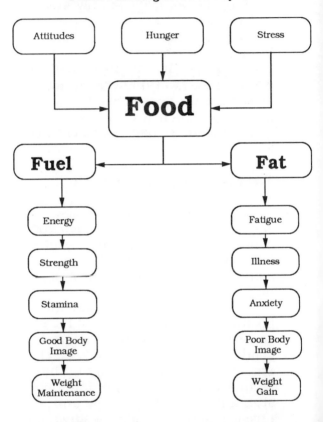

Figure 7

If we approach food from the negative motivations of reducing stress, replacing love, or avoiding anxiety, we will seek out foods that seem to satisfy those needs, however temporarily — foods that are almost invariably high in sugars and calories and low in real food value. They will produce fat, which in turn will produce fatigue, illness, and excess weight. These will result in depression, low self-esteem, more anxiety and stress, and poor body image, and *that* leads us to seek out more of those false foods and continue the negative cycle.

It is our basic beliefs about food that get us into trouble in the first place, and it is our basic beliefs about food that we must change if we are to change our eating patterns and habits. And this is the only thing that will change our body weight permanently.

A balanced food plan from a balanced life

Let's look at Figures 8 and 9 for a moment. Figure 8 presents a symmetrical, balanced group of the ways available to us to satisfy our basic needs. As you can see, we use a variety of activities, people, and things, including food, to satisfy the basic needs of a full human being. And because each of us is unique, there's a box for something that works for you personally that may not work for others.

You may want to play a little personal game of tic-tac-toe here. Put a button or a dime or something on the boxes that you actively use in your life. If all nine boxes have at least one button, you're probably living a pretty balanced life. If some boxes have nothing and other boxes have two or three buttons, it's a sure sign that you could use some adjustment.

Figure 9 shows us very graphically and powerfully what happens when food becomes the dominant satisfier. All the other boxes get squeezed and minimized. And if food is heavily abused and takes over a person's life as a dominant compulsion, some boxes would be eliminated altogether. Many people give up exercise and hobbies and, sadly, even friends and love.

Balanced Needs / Satisfaction Grid

Love	Work	Friends
Hobbies	Family	Service
Exercise	Your Personal Method	Food

Figure 8

Unbalanced Needs / Satisfaction Grid

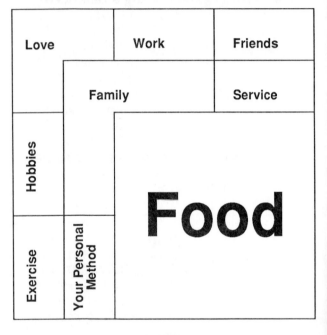

Figure 9

A good food plan that leads to a healthy and appropriate body weight for you will naturally become a part of an overall good life plan that has you living a balanced, energetic, joyful, loving life.

As you change your basic beliefs and attitudes about food, you'll also, very naturally, change your basic beliefs and attitudes about many other areas of your life. For instance, suppose part of your present eating pattern is to sit, mesmerized, in front of the TV, eating sweets and snacks just to avoid or relieve anxiety. As you change that eating pattern and learn to do something else about the anxiety, you may find yourself watching less TV. Another eating pattern may be that you isolate yourself because of embarrassment about what you eat or the way you eat. As you change those patterns, you'll find yourself spending more time with friends.

How our poor habits are encouraged

It's not enough that we developed these poor attitudes with

great help from others. We are constantly encouraged to maintain and expand them. We are literally marketed to death. We are encouraged and motivated and prodded to stuff our bodies with a wide assortment of sweets and fats and other things that maintain the negative loop of feeling bad and eating more in a useless attempt to try to feel better.

"Feeling low? Drink this and join the fun." "Need a midday pick-me-up? Eat this and finish the job and get the promotion and go on to be company president." Companies have a right to do this. It is, after all, how they make their money. And you have a right — more, an obligation — to say *no!*

You may have to battle your way up from very deep habits of eating poorly and non-nutritionally. But if you stay with your program, you're almost certain to gain results. You have a goal, a new vision. A new, healthier, more energetic you. You're doing the most powerful thing you can do. You are working at changing your basic beliefs and attitudes about food. Remember that some of these ideas are as old as you are and that they are constantly reinforced by the TV and print media.

Be gentle and loving with yourself. Allow the changes to come gradually, clearly, permanently. Your old attitudes and beliefs, because they've been around for so long and are so entrenched and are constantly reinforced, speak with very loud voices, accustomed to obedience.

As you undergo your changes you'll begin to hear a new voice. At first it will be a gentle, vulnerable whisper that you'll have to pay very special attention just to hear at all. You'll have to listen for the voice. Invite it to speak up. Give it extra attention in the beginning, just as you would a new member of the family, who is timid and shy and not used to being heard.

Subliminal tapes (those that are well-designed and carefully manufactured) are specially created to give life to this new voice, to give you a new way to look at and think about food. The need for a quick midafternoon pick-me-up is usually answered by the old voice booming, "Have some ice cream, a candy bar, or some donuts." The new voice will suggest, "A nice, cold apple would really taste good right now." Listen. With practice and attention your attitudes and beliefs will change. Then your actions will change. You'll develop new food habits and change into a new, slimmer, healthier, more energetic you.

Appendix B
The Institute for Subliminal Studies

The field of subliminal learning is constantly expanding. One major lesson we learned while researching this book is that subliminal learning is an exciting, challenging new field, full of promise and possibilities. Not a week goes by that we don't get some new company, new products, or a new study keeping us right on the very edge of developments.

We have formed the Institute for Subliminal Studies as a focal point, a clearinghouse, to gather, analyze, interpret, and share information.

The Institute is designed to

- Stay current with research and experimentation

- Evaluate and test new products as they emerge

- Issue special reports, newsletters, and statement papers

- Maintain a special research track to follow the evolution of subliminal products and the law

- Receive, log, evaluate, and report on all correspondence from individual users of subliminal products — successes and misses.

Whether you are a company or an individual, please share your experiences and projections with us so that we may in turn perform the service of sharing them with others.

Write to

The Institute for Subliminal Studies
P.O. Box 1018
Santa Monica, CA 90406-1018
Phone: 213-394-4102
Fax: 213-394-2603
1-800-669-0409

Appendix C
Manufacturers and Their Products

Here is a list of manufacturers of subliminal products. We did our best to include every company we became aware of while researching this book. Some companies we called to try to gather information didn't respond. We have no way of knowing whether they are no longer in the subliminal business or maybe just never got back to us, but if they didn't get back to us, they might not get back to you. The companies listed here at least responded with their catalogs and other literature — some of it quite informative about subliminals. We urge you to write or call these companies to gather as much information as you can (especially about guarantees) so you can make the best purchases possible.

If you are an active manufacturer of subliminal products and your company is not listed here, please write to us care of the publisher or the Institute for Subliminal Studies, and we'll be sure to list you in future editions of this book.

Alphasonics • 12228 Venice Blvd., Suite 501 • Los Angeles, CA 90066 • 213-301-1849

Audio Additions • P.O. Box 6930 • Auburn, CA 95604 • 800-231-4261, fax 916-888-7805

Audio Renaissance Tapes, Inc. • 9110 Sunset Blvd., Suite 240 • Los Angeles, CA 90069 • 213-939-1840, fax 213-935-9986

Conscious Living Foundation • P.O. Box 9 • Drain, OR 97435 • 800-752-2256

CSI • P.O. Box 244 • Aurora, CO 80040

Effective Learning Systems, Inc. • The Love Tapes • 5221 Industrial Blvd. • Edina, MN 55435 • 612-893-1680

Escott International, Inc. • 2000 Oakley Park Rd., Suite 104 • Walled Lake, MI 48088 • 800-433-2291

Gateways Research Institute • P.O. Box 41 • Ojai, CA 93023 • 800-777-8908, 805-646-8148

Hazelden Educational Materials • P.O. Box 176 • Pleasant Valley Rd. • Center City, MN 55012-0176 • 800-328-9000, in MN 800-257-0070, 612-257-4010

Helioscience Institute • 1324 San Andres St. • Santa Barbara, CA 93101 • 800-248-1244 (at the tone, dial 7295)

Joe Land Co., The • P.O. Box 11371 • Albuquerque NM 87192 • 800-468-2700

John-David Learning Institute, Inc. • 2443 Impala Drive • Carlsbad, CA 92008-3873 • 800-437-5646, in CA 800-624-9779, 619-931-0456

Light of Mind Publishing • P.O. Box 280 • Topanga, CA 90290 • 800-824-4000, ext. 1016; 818-992-0880

Mind Communication, Inc. • P.O. Box 904 • 1844 Porter, S.W. • Grand Rapids, MI 49509-0429 • 800-237-1974, in MI 616-531-9972

Nightingale-Conant Corporation • 7300 North Lehigh Ave. • Chicago, IL 60648 • 800-323-5552, fax 312-647-7145

Potentials Unlimited, Inc. • P.O. Box 891 • Grand Rapids, MI 49518 • 800-426-3963

Psychodynamics Research Institute • Western Office • P.O. Box 875 • Zephyr Cove, NV 89448 • 800-654-6999, 702-588-7999

Stillpoint Publishing • P.O. Box 640 • Walpole, NH 03608 • 800-847-4014, in NH 603-756-4225

Success Education Institute International • The Randolph Tapes • P.O. Box 90608 • 2108 Garnet Ave. • San Diego, CA 92109-3603 • 800-248-2737, 619-276-9800, fax 619-273-0813

Valley of the Sun Publishing Co. • P.O. Box 3004 • Agoura Hills, CA 91301 • 800-421-6603, in CA 800-225-4717, 818-889-1575

Appendix D
References and Further Reading

Here is a listing of the journal articles and reports we've found to be available and of interest on the subject of subliminal learning. While this is an extensive list, we know that there is more work than this going on. Also, there are many newspaper and trade magazine articles, which refer to subliminal learning and which we read for general background, that we did not include here. We considered their references too general and spotty to be of serious use to anyone wanting to do more reading on the subject.

You'll find most of the works listed here available in the main library of your community or the local college or university. For some of the journals you may need the assistance of your research librarian. Take heart. They're trained to locate the difficult and usually take great pleasure in doing so.

If you are the author of some work we didn't reference here, please let us know and send us a copy of your work to the Institute for Subliminal Studies. If you're currently working on an experiment or a project, please let us know what you're working on so that we might allow room to discuss it as it applies to our coverage in subsequent editions of this book.

Ariam-S. Siller-J. Effects of subliminal oneness stimuli in Hebrew on academic performance of Israeli high school students: further evidence on the adaptation-enhancing effects of symbiotic fantasies in another culture using another language. J-Abnorm-Psychol. 1982 Oct. 91(5). P 343-9.

Bagby-P-K. The effect of symbiotic and oedipal subliminal stimuli on field independence and competitive tasks. Dissertation Abstracts International. 1985 Jun vol 45(12-b, pt 1) 3927.

Balay-J. Shevrin-H. The subliminal psychodynamic activation method: a critical review. American Psychologist. 1988 Mar vol 43(3) 161-174.

Balay-J-S. The role of aggression in bipolar affective disorder: a subliminal approach. Dissertation Abstracts International. 1987 Oct vol 48(4-b) 1145.

Baldwin-RB. Kinetic art - use of subliminal stimulation of visual perception. Leonardo. 1974, V7 n1. P1-5.

Barchas-P-R. Perlaki-K-M. Processing of preconsciously acquired information measured by hemispheric asymmetry and selection accuracy. Behav-Neurosci. 1986 Jun. 100(3). P 343-9.

Bargh-J-A. Bond-R-N. Lombardi-W-J. Tota-M-E. The additive nature of chronic and temporary sources of construct accessibility. Journal of Personality & Social Psychology. 1986 May vol 50(5) 869-878.

Bauer-W-D. The effects of conditional and unconditional subliminal symbiotic stimuli on intrinsic motivation. Dissertation Abstracts International. 1986 Feb vol 46(8-b) 2794-2795.

Bell-P-D. The interspersal technique of Milton Erickson: testing an operational definition. Dissertation Abstracts International. 1986 Apr vol 46 (10-b) 3586-3587.

Berg-D. "Transformers," Barbie dolls and the Cabbage Patch Kids: toys, technology, and human identity. Etc. 1986 Sum vol 43(2) 207-211.

Bernstein-B-R. The effects of subliminal symbiotic and oedipal stimuli on weight loss in obese women. Dissertation Abstracts International. 1986 Feb vol 46(8-b) 2795.

Berry-D-M. Effects of educative/support groups and subliminal psychodynamic activation on bulimia in college women. Dissertation Abstracts International. 1985 May vol 45(11-b) 3612.

Block-M-P. Vanden-Bergh-B-G. Can you sell subliminal messages to consumers? Journal of Advertising. 1985 Vol 14(3) 59-62.

Borgeat-F. Goulet-J. Psychophysiological changes following auditory subliminal suggestions for activation and deactivation. Perceptual & Motor Skills. 1983 Jun vol 56(3) 759-766.

Borgeat-F. Chaloult-L. A relaxation experiment using radio broadcasts. Canada's Mental Health. 1985 Mar vol 33(1) 11-13.

Borgeat-F. Pannetier-M-F. Value of cumulative electrodermal responses in subliminal auditory perception. A preliminary study. Encephale. 1982. 8(4). P 487-99.

Borgeat-F. Elie-R. Chaloult-L. Chabot-R. Psychophysiological responses to masked auditory stimuli. Canadian Journal of Psychiatry. 1985 Feb vol 30 (1) 22-27.

Borgeat-F. Psychophysiological effects of two different relaxation procedures: progressive relaxation and subliminal relaxation. Psychiatric Journal of the University of Ottawa. 1983 Dec vol 8(4) 181-185.

Bornstein-R-F. Subliminal mere exposure effects and conscious cognition: a study of attitude changes in response to stimuli perceived without awareness. Dissertation Abstracts International. 1987 Mar vol 47(9-b) 3941.

Bornstein-R-F. Leone-D-R. Galley-D-J. The generalizability of subliminal mere exposure effects: influence of stimuli perceived without awareness on social behavior. Special issue: integrating personality and social psychology. Journal of Personality & Social Psychology. 1987 Dec vol 53(6) 1070-1079.

Bouchard-S-J. Effects of a self-administered subliminal-relaxation treatment on anxiety. Dissertation Abstracts International. 1984 Dec vol 45 (6-b) 1906.

Bovier-P. Broekkamp-C-L. Lloyd-K-G. Enhancing GABAergic transmission reverses the aversive state in rats induced by electrical stimulation of the periaqueductal grey region. Brain-Res. 1982 Sep 30. 248(2). P 313-20.

Brandeis-D. Lehmann-D. Event-related potentials of the brain and cognitive processes: approaches and applications. Special issue: methods in neuropsychology. Neuropsychologia. 1986 Vol 24(1) 151-168.

Brennan-S-M. The effect of subliminal separation-individuation schemas on moral reasoning and mood in depressed and non-depressed women. Dissertation Abstracts International. 1984 Dec vol 45(6-b) 1907.

Bromfield-R-N. Subliminal psychodynamic activation: demonstration, oedipal factors and personality correlates. Dissertation Abstracts International. 1986 May vol 46(11-b) 4005.

Bronstein-A-A. Rodin-G-C. An experimental study of internalization fantasies in schizophrenic men. Psychotherapy: Theory, Research & Practice. 1983 Win vol 20(4) 408-416.

Bryant-T-R. Silverman-L-H. Effects of the subliminal stimulation of symbiotic fantasies on the academic performance of emotionally handicapped students. Journal of Counseling Psychology. 1984 Jul vol 31(3) 295-305.

Caracciolo-D. Shirsat-N. Wong-G-G. Lange-B. Clark-S. Rovera-G. Recombinant human macrophage colony-stimulating factor (M-CSF) requires subliminal concentrations of granulocyte/macrophage (GM)-CSF for optimal stimulation of human macrophage colony formation in vitro. J-Exp-Med. 1987 Dec 1. 166(6). P 1851-60.

Carlsson-I. Smith-G-J. Gender differences in defense mechanisms compared with creativity in a group of youngsters. Psychological Research Bulletin, Lund U. 1987 Vol 27(1)(26(1) sic) 20 p.

Carlsson-I. Smith-G-J. Identification with an aggressor or a victim and its relation to creativity. Scandinavian Journal of Psychology. 1986 Vol 27(3) 252-257.

Castricone-L-E. Effects of subliminal symbiotic activation on empathy as measured by conceptual level of object representation, cognitive decentering, and drive content. Dissertation Abstracts International. 1987 Oct vol 48 (4-b) 1141.

Cheesman-J. Merikle-P-M. Priming with and without awareness. Perception & Psychophysics. 1984 Oct vol 36 (4) 387-395.

Cheesman-J-E. Distinguishing conscious from unconscious perceptual processes. Dissertation Abstracts International. 1987 Apr vol 47(10-b) 4335.

Chimera-D-M. An exploration of the effect of auditory subliminal stimuli on schizophrenic pathology. Dissertation Abstracts International. 1987 Nov vol 48(5-b) 1509.

Chinen-A-B. Spielvogel-A-M. Farrell-D. The experience of intuition. Psychological Perspectives. 1985 Fal vol 16(2) 186-197.

Clark-M-M. Effects of social support and subliminal stimulation on anxiety reduction. Dissertation Abstracts International. 1987 Jul vol 48(1-b) 258.

Clark-M-M. Procidano-me. Comparison of the effectiveness of subliminal stimulation and social support on anxiety reduction. Social Behavior and Personality. 1987, V15 n2. P177-183.

Conte-M. Gennaro-A. Percezione inconscia, percezione subliminale, attivazione psicodinamica subliminale: itinerari e metodi. (Unconscious perceptions, subliminal perceptions, and subliminal psychodynamic activation: paths and methodologies.). Giornale Storico di Psicologia Dinamica. 1983 Jan vol 7(13) 134-158.

Cook-H. Effects of subliminal symbiotic gratification and the magic of believing on achievement. Psychoanalytic Psychology. 1985 Fal vol 2(4) 365-371.

Cooper-C. Kline-P. An evaluation of the defence mechanism test. British Journal of Psychology. 1986 Feb vol 77(1) 19-32.

Crawford-B-H. Palmer-D-A. The scotopic visibility curve and cone intrusion. Vision Research. 1985 Vol 25(6) 863-866.

Cuperfain-R. Clarke-T-K. A new perspective of subliminal perception. Journal of Advertising. 1985 Vol 14(1) 36-41.

Czyzewska-P-M. Zjawisko primingu w pamieci semantycznej wywolane przez bodzce podprogowe. / The priming phenomenon in semantic memory evoked by sub-threshold stimuli. Przeglad Psychologiczny. 1984 Vol 27 (3) 617-629.

Dauber-R-B. Subliminal psychodynamic activation in depression: on the role of autonomy issues in depressed college women. Journal of Abnormal Psychology. 1984 Feb vol 93(1) 9-18.

Davidson-C. Derkert-T. Manligtkvinnligt. Kastrationsangestens roll vid masochistisk och narcissistisk problematik. (Male-female: the role of castration anxiety in masochistic and narcissistic problems.) Psykisk Halsa. 1985 Vol 26(2) 86-92.

Deviatkina-T-A. Tarasenko-L-M. B byreva-L-E. Sergienko-N-G. Voskresenskii-O-N. Lipid peroxidation in tissues during subliminal electrostimulation of limbic system structures in the brain. Biull-Eksp-Biol-Med. 1985 Oct. 100(10). P 412-4.

Dixon-N-F. The conscious-unconscious interface: contributions to an understanding. Arch-Psychol (Frankf). 1983. 135(1). P 55-66.

Dixon-N-F. Henley-S-H. Weir-C-G. Extraction of information from continuously masked successive stimuli: an exploratory study. Current Psychological Research & Reviews. 1984 Spr vol 3 (1) 38-44.

Draguns-J-G. Why microgenesis? An inquiry on the motivational sources of going beyond the information given. Arch-Psychol (Frankf). 1983. 135(1). P 5-16.

Erdley-C-A. Dagostino-P-R. Cognitive and affective components of automatic priming effects. Journal of Personality & Social Psychology. 1988 May vol 54 (5) 741-747.

Firestone-R-W. The "inner voice" and suicide. Psychotherapy. 1986 Fal vol 23(3) 439-447.

Fisher-C. Further observations on the Poetzl phenomenon: the effects of subliminal visual stimulation on dreams, images, and hallucinations. Psychiatric Evolution Group (1958, Paris, France). Psychoanalysis & Contemporary Thought. 1988 Vol 11(1) 3-56.

Fisher-C-B. Glenwick-D-S. Blumenthal-R-S. Subliminal oedipal stimuli and competitive performance: an investigation of between-groups effects and mediating subject variables. Journal of Abnormal Psychology. 1986 g vol 95(3) 292-294.

Florek-W-G. An investigation of the effects of stimulating symbiotic fantasies in primipara females. Dissertation Abstracts International. 1985 Nov vol 46(5-b) 1720.

Frauman-D-C. Lynn-S-J. Hardaway-R. Molteni-A. Effect of subliminal symbiotic activation on hypnotic rapport and susceptibility. Journal of Abnormal Psychology. 1984 Nov vol 93(4) 481-483.

Froufe-T-M. Sierra-D-B. Percepcion sin conciencia. (Perception without awareness.). Boletin de Psicologia (Spain). 1985 Jun no 7 7-50.

Fudin-R. Subliminal psychodynamic activation: Mommy and I are not yet one. Perceptual & Motor Skills. 1986 Dec vol 63(3) 1159-1179.

Fudin-R. Subliminal psychodynamic activation: note on illumination and the bleaching hypothesis. Perceptual & Motor Skills. 1987 Jun vol 64(3, pt 2) 1223-1230.

Fudin-R. Response to Weinberger's comments on "subliminal psychodynamic activation: Mommy and I are not yet one." Perceptual & Motor Skills. 1987 Apr vol 64(2) 639-642.

Gable-M. Wilkens-H-T. Harris-L. Feinberg-R. An evaluation of subliminally embedded sexual stimuli in graphics. Journal of Advertising. 1987 Vol 16(1) 26-31.

Gaethke-Brandt-J-E. The effect of auditory subliminal deactivating messages on motor and task performance of hyperkinetic children. Dissertation Abstracts International. 1986 Oct vol 47(4-a) 1184.

Geisler-C. The use of subliminal psychodynamic activation in the study of repression. Journal of Personality & Social Psychology. 1986 Oct vol 51(4) 844-851.

Genkina-O-A. Shostakovich-G-S. Elaboration of a conditioned reflex in chronic alcoholics using an unrecognizable motivationally significant word. Zh-Vyssh-Nerv-Deiat. 1983 Nov-Dec. 33(6). P 1010-8.

Genkina-O-A. Shostakovich-G-S. Cortical evoked activity in the process of elaborating a conditioned connection using an unrecognizable word. Fiziol-Cheloveka. 1987 May-Jun. 13(3). P 369-78.

Genkina-O-A. Shostakovich-G-S. Conditioning of patients with chronic alcoholism by means of a subthreshold motivationally significant word. Soviet Neurology & Psychiatry. 1986 Sum vol 19(2) 87-100.

Gessaga-E-C. Herrick-M-K. Urich-H. Necrosis of the fetal brain stem with cerebellar hypoplasia. Acta-Neuropathol (Berl). 1986. 69(3-4). P 326-31.

Glover-ED. Decreasing smoking-behavior through subliminal stimulation treatments. Journal of Drug Education. 1979, V9 n3. P273-283.

Goncalves-O-F. Ivey-A-E. The effects of unconscious presentation of information on therapist conceptualizations, intentions, and responses. Journal of Clinical Psychology. 1987 Mar vol 43(2) 237-245.

Gonzalez-JL. Subliminal stimulation and psychopathologic diagnosis. Psiquis. 1985, V6 n1. P30+.

Groeger-J-A. Preconscious influences on word substitutions. Irish Journal of Psychology. 1986 Fal vol 7(2) 88-97.

Groeger-J-A. Evidence of unconscious semantic processing from a forced error situation. Br-J-Psychol. 1984 Aug. 75 (Pt 3). P 305-14.

Groeger-J-A. Predominant and nonpredominant analysis: effects of level of presentation. British Journal of Psychology. 1986 Feb vol 77(1) 109-116.

Hardaway-R-A. Facts and fantasies in subliminal psychodynamic activation: a qualitative analysis. Dissertation Abstracts International. 1987 Jun vol 47(12-b, pt 1) 5054.

Hary-D. Moore-G-P. Synchronizing human movement with an external clock source. Biol-Cybern. 1987. 56 (5-6). P 305-11.

Haspel-K-C. Harris-R-S. Effect of tachistoscopic stimulation of subconscious oedipal wishes on competitive performance: a failure to replicate. J-Abnorm-Psychol. 1982 Dec. 91(6). P 437-43.

Hodorowski-L. The symbiotic fantasy as a therapeutic agent: an experimental comparison of the effects of four symbiotic contexts on manifest pathology in differentiated schizophrenics. Dissertation Abstracts International. 1986 Feb vol 46(8-b) 2810.

Hovsepian-W. Quatman-G. Effects of subliminal stimulation on masculinity-femininity ratings of a male model. Perceptual and Motor Skills. 1978, V46 n1. P155-161.

Hubbard-G-M. Licht-P. In vitro ovarian responses to pulsatile and continuous gonadotrophin administration on steroid secretion and oocyte maturation in the frogs, Rana pipiens and Rana catesbeiana. Gen-Comp-Endocrinol. 1986 Mar. 61(3). P 417-23.

Jackson-JM. Effects of subliminal stimulation of oneness fantasies on manifest pathology in male vs female schizophrenics. Journal of Nervous & Mental Disease. 1983, V171 n5. P280-289.

Kaplan-R. Thornton-P. Silverman-L. Further data on the effects of subliminal symbiotic stimulation on schizophrenics. Journal of Nervous & Mental Disease. 1985 Nov vol 173(11) 658-666.

Kaser-V-A. The effects of an auditory subliminal message upon the production of images and dreams. Journal of Nervous & Mental Disease. 1986 Jul vol 174(7) 397-407.

Kemp-Wheeler-S-M. Hill-A-B. Anxiety responses to subliminal experience of mild stress. Br-J-Psychol. 1987 Aug. 78 (Pt 3). P 365-74.

Kihlstrom-J-F. The cognitive unconscious. Science. 1987 Sep 18. 237 (4821). P 1445-52.

Kilbourne-W-E. Painton-S. Ridley-D. The effect of sexual embedding on responses to magazine advertisements. Journal of Advertising. 1985 Vol 14(2) 48-55.

Kim-J-O. Rhee-K. Cho-J-R. Semantic information processing of Korean words. Korean Journal of Psychology. 1984 Fal vol 4(3) 185-200.

Kirkwood-B-J. Subliminal control of behaviour: myth or miracle? N-Z-Med-J. 1987 Feb 11. 100(817). P 69-70.

Kleinbrook-W-L. Pastoral considerations regarding the use of subliminal psychodynamic activation. Dissertation Abstracts International. 1985 Feb vol 45(8-a) 2555.

Kostandov-E-A. Current significance of the work of G. V. Gershuni on subsensory reactions. Zh-Vyssh-Nerv-Deiat. 1985 Nov-Dec. 35(6). P 1014-21.

Kostandov-E-A. Arzumanov-YuL. The influence of subliminal emotional words on functional hemispheric asymmetry. Int-J-Psychophysiol. 1986 Jul. 4(2). P 143-7.

Koufopoulos-R-M. A study of introjective depression using the subliminal psychodynamic activation method. Dissertation Abstracts International. 1987 Sep vol 48(3-b) 880.

Krishna-S-R. A review of the pan-india conference. Journal of Parapsychology. 1985 Sep vol 49(3) 249-255.

Kunzendorf-R-G. Lacourse-P. Lynch-B. Hypnotic hypermnesia for subliminally encoded stimuli: state-dependent memory for "unmonitored" sensations. Imagination, Cognition & Personality. 1986-87 Vol 6(4) 365-377.

Ladouceur-R. Mercier-P. Awareness: an understudied cognitive factor in behavior therapy. Psychol-Rep. 1984 Feb. 54(1). P 159-78.

Langerholc-J. Che cos'ha da sorridere, veramente, la signora? Gli ammiratori segreti di monna lisa. (Trans c. C. Bakargiev) (What is the Mona Lisa really smiling about?). Rivista di Psicologia dell'Arte. 1984 Jun-Dec vol 6(10-11) 5-22.

Lee-I. Tyrer-P. Horn-S. A comparison of subliminal, supraliminal and faded phobic cine-films in the treatment of agoraphobia. British Journal of Psychiatry. 1983 Oct vol 143 356-361.

Leuschner-W. Acoustic method of experimental dream stimulation. Psyche (Stuttg). 1986 Apr. 40(4). P 341-54.

Levy-M-A. The intimacy motive: a variable to predict responsiveness to subliminal symbiotic stimulation. Dissertation Abstracts International. 1985 Jan vol 45(7-b) 2314.

Lewis-A-J. Parker-J. DiLuigi-J. Datko-L-J. Carlson-R-P. Immunomodulation of delayed hypersensitivity to methylated bovine serum albumin (MBSA) in mice using subliminal and normal sensitization procedures. J-Immunopharmacol. 1981-82. 3(3-4). P 289-307.

Lindeman-M-L. Suggestion in education: the historical path of suggestopedia. Journal of Evolutionary Psychology. 1985 Mar vol 6(1-2) 107-118.

Linehan-E. Otoole-J. Effect of subliminal stimulation of symbiotic fantasies on college-student self-disclosure in group-counseling. Journal of Counseling Psychology. 1982, V29 n2. P151-157.

Lorenzo-Gonzalez-J. Estimulacion subliminal y diagnostico psicopatologico. (Subliminal stimulation and psychopathologic diagnosis.) Psiquis: Revista de Psiquiatria, Psicologia y Psicosomatica. 1985 Jan-feb vol 6(1) 30-40.

Lorenzo-Gonzalez-J. Influencia de la estimulacion subliminal en la percepcion. (Influence of subliminal stimulation on perception.) Revista de Psicologia General y Aplicada. 1985 Vol 40(5) 1019-1031.

Lynn-Ronald-L. Relaxation: low-intensity (subliminal) phrases versus instructional set. Dissertation Abstracts International. 1987 Sep vol 48 (3-b) 882.

Manfield-D-C. Computer-assisted weight-loss: a subliminal and behavioral methodology for motivated females. Dissertation Abstracts International. 1987 Mar vol 47(9-b) 3943.

Marcel-A-J. Conscious and unconscious perception: experiments on visual masking and word recognition. Cognit-Psychol. 1983 Apr. 15(2). P 197-237.

Mcgreen-P-J. The effects of father absence on affective responses to subliminal symbiotic messages. Dissertation Abstracts International. 1986 May vol 46(11-b) 4021-4022.

McIlwraith-R-D. Community mental health and the mass media in Canada. Canada's Mental Health. 1987 Sep vol 35(3) 11-17.

Mendelsohn-M. An investigation of the relationship between the symbiotic subliminal stimulus Mommy and I are one and oral receptivity and oral aggressivity as measured by the Rorschach test. Dissertation Abstracts International. 1984 Nov vol 45(5-b) 1601-1602.

Miller-L. In search of the unconscious. Psychology Today.
1986 Dec vol 20(12) 60-64.

Mitchell-M-S. The effects of subliminally presented praise and reprobation stimuli on willingness to self-disclose. Dissertation Abstracts International. 1985 Jun vol 45(12-b, pt 1) 3986.

Mofield-J-P. Response of blood pressure to relaxation and subliminal suggestion. Dissertation Abstracts International. 1986 Mar vol 46(9-a) 2632.

Moroney-E. Bross-M. Effect of subliminal visual material on an auditory signal detection task. Percept-Mot-Skills. 1984 Feb. 58(1). P 103-13.

Nash-M-R. Lynn-S-J. Stanley-S. Carlson-V. Subjectively complete hypnotic deafness and auditory priming. International Journal of Clinical & Experimental Hypnosis. 1987 Jan vol 35(1) 32-40.

Nash-C-B. Comparison of subliminal and extrasensory perception. Journal of the Society for Psychical Research. 1986 Oct vol 53(805) 435-455.

Neumarkt-P. The Ezra Pound issue: a psychological assessment. Journal of Evolutionary Psychology. 1987 Aug vol 8(3-4) 187-190.

Niedenthal-P-M. Unconscious affect in social cognition.
Dissertation Abstracts International. 1988 Jan vol 48(7-b) 2143.

Ofman-P-S. Effects of sexual and aggressive subliminal stimulation on response to sexual and aggressive humor. Dissertation Abstracts International. 1988 Jan vol 48(7-b) 2105.

Oliver-J-M. Burkham-R. "Comments on three recent subliminal psychodynamic activation investigations": reply to Silverman. Journal of Abnormal Psychology. 1985 Nov vol 94(4) 644.

Oliver-J-M. Burkham-R. Subliminal psychodynamic activation in depression: a failure to replicate. J-Abnorm-Psychol. 1982 Oct. 91(5). P 337-42.

Olson-J-M. Misattribution, preparatory information, and speech anxiety. Journal of Personality & Social Psychology. 1988 May vol 54(5) 758-767.

Overbeeke-C-J. Changing the perception of behavioral properties by subliminal presentation. Perceptual & Motor Skills. 1986 Feb vol 62(1) 255-258.

Palmatier-JR. Bornstein-PH. Effects of subliminal stimulation of symbiotic merging fantasies on behavioral treatment of smokers. Journal of Nervous and Mental Disease. 1980, V168 n12. P715-720.

Palumbo-R. Gillman-Irene. Effects of subliminal activation of oedipal fantasies on competitive performance: a replication and extension. Journal of Nervous and Mental Disease. 1984 Dec vol 172(12) 737-741.

Parks-T-E. Illusory figures, illusory objects, and real objects. Psychological Review. 1986 Apr vol 93(2) 207-215.

Patton-C-J. Bulimia and depression: a subliminal psychodynamic activation investigation. Dissertation Abstracts International. 1988 Apr vol 48(10-b) 3118.

Porterfield-A-L. "Comments on three recent subliminal psychodynamic activation investigations": reply to Silverman. Journal of Abnormal Psychology. 1985 Nov vol 94(4) 645-646.

Porterfield-A-L. Golding-S-L. Failure to find an effect of subliminal psychodynamic activation upon cognitive measures of pathology in schizophrenia. Journal of Abnormal Psychology. 1985 Nov vol 94(4) 630-639.

Rao-P-V. Vindhya-S-U. The differential effect as a psi-sensory relationship. Journal of the Society for Psychical Research. 1987 Jul vol 54(808) 181-185.

Robles-R. Smith-R. Carver-C-S. Wellens-A-R. Influence of subliminal visual images on the experience of anxiety. Personality & Social Psychology Bulletin. 1987 Sep vol 13(3) 399-410.

Roll-W-G. De-a-Montagno-E. System theory, neurophysiology and psi. International conference on parapsychology: Eastern and Western perspectives (1985, Waltair, India). Journal of Indian Psychology. 1985 Jul vol 4(2) 43-84.

Roney-Dougal-S-M. Subliminal and psi perception: a review of the literature. Journal of the Society for Psychical Research. 1986 Oct vol 53(805) 405-434.

Roney-Dougal-S-M. A comparison of psi and subliminal perception: exploratory and follow-up studies. Journal of the American Society for Psychical Research. 1987 Apr vol 81(2) 141-181.

Roseman-J. The role of subliminal messages and sensation-seeking in eating restraint of the obese and non-obese. Dissertation Abstracts International. 1985 Aug vol 46(2-b) 659.

Roth-N. Roscher-G. Heine-A. Memory recall after "subliminal" stimuli: a psychophysiological analysis. Act-Nerv-Super (Praha). 1988 Jun. 30(2). P 130-2.

Schurtman-R. Palmatier-J-R. Martin-E-S. On the activation of symbiotic gratification fantasies as an aid in the treatment of alcoholics. Int-J-Addict. 1982 Oct. 17(7). P 1157-74.

Shevrin-H. Brain wave correlates of subliminal stimulation, unconscious attention, primary- and secondary-process thinking, and repressiveness. Psychological Issues. 1973, V8 n2. P56-87.

Shevrin-H. Subliminal perception and dreaming. Special issue: cognition and dream research. Journal of Mind & Behavior. 1986 Spr-sum vol 7(2-3) 379-395.

Shostakovich-G-S. Neurologic mechanism of the unconscious craving for alcohol in chronic alcoholic patients. Zh-Nevropatol-Psikhiatr. 1987. 87(6). P 898-902.

Silverman-L-H. Lachmann-F-M. The therapeutic properties of unconscious oneness fantasies: evidence and treatment implications. Contemporary Psychoanalysis. 1985 Jan vol 21(1) 91-115.

Silverman-LH. Martin-A. Ungaro-R. Mendelsohn-E. Effect of subliminal stimulation of symbiotic fantasies on behavior-modification treatment of obesity. Journal of Consulting and Clinical Psychology. 1978, V46 n3. P432-441.

Silverman-L-H. "Comments on three recent subliminal psychodynamic activation investigations": rejoinder to Oliver and Burkham and to Porterfield. Journal of Abnormal Psychology. 1985 Nov vol 94(4) 647-648.

Silverman-L-H. Weinberger-J. Mommy and I are one: implications for psychotherapy. American Psychologist. 1985 Dec vol 40(12) 1296-1308.

Silverman-L-H. Research on psychoanalytic psychodynamic propositions. Special issue: current thinking in psychoanalysis. Clinical Psychology Review. 1985 Vol 5(3) 247-257.

Smith-G-J. Carlsson-I. Danielsson-A. Identification with another person: manipulated by means of subliminal stimulation. Scandinavian Journal of Psychology. 1985 Vol 26(1) 74-87.

Smith-G-J. Carlsson-I. Sandstrom-S. Artists and artistic creativity-elucidated by psychological experiments. Psychological Research Bulletin, Lund U. 1985 Vol 25(9-10) 26 p.

Smith-G-J. Carlsson-I. Creativity and anxiety: an experimental study. Scand-J-Psychol. 1983. 24(2). P 107-15.

Smith-G. Carlsson-I. Depressive retardation and subliminally manipulated aggressive involvement. Psychological Research Bulletin, Lund U. 1987 Vol 27(5) 14 p.

Smith-F-E. Does your writing send the wrong signals? Personnel Journal. 1985 Dec vol 64(12) 28-30.

Smith-G-J. Carlsson-I. Creativity and aggression.
Psychoanalytic Psychology. 1986 Spr vol 3(2) 159-172.

Soininen-K. Jarvilehto-T. Somatosensory evoked potentials associated with tactile stimulation at detection threshold in man. Electroencephalogr-Clin-Neurophysiol. 1983 Nov. 56(5). P 494-500.

Sommer-L. The effects of subliminal psychodynamic activation on verbal time estimation. Dissertation Abstracts International. 1986 Mar vol 46 (9-b) 3231.

Spence-D-P. Subliminal effects on lexical decision time.
Arch-Psychol (Frankf). 1983. 135(1). P 67-72.

Stambrook-M. Martin-D-G. Brain laterality and the subliminal perception of facial expression. Int-J-Neurosci. 1983. 18(1-2). P 45-58.

Thornton-P-I. Igleheart-HC. Silverman-LH. Subliminal stimulation of symbiotic fantasies as an aid in the treatment of drug-abusers. International Journal of the Addictions. 1987, V22 n8. P751-765.

Thornton-J-W. A test of subliminal symbiotic activation as a means of alleviating depression. Psychoanalytic Psychology. 1987 Fal vol 4(4) 335-342.

Thuerer-J-R. Computer-assisted spelling: a subliminal methodology to increase cognitive performance and academic self-concept. Dissertation Abstracts International. 1985 Apr vol 45(10-a) 3074.

Trebenok-Z-A. Soldatenkov-V-A. Sorokina-N-I. Filippovich-I-V. Role of hypoxanthine in the radiation death of thymocytes in vitro. Radiobiologiia. 1985 Jul-Aug. 25(4). P 521-4.

Treimer-M. Simonson-M. Subliminal messages, persuasion, and behavior change. J-Soc-Psychol. 1988 Aug. 128 (4). P 563-5.

Tricou-C-F. A study of the effects of auditory subliminal stimulation upon male versus female sixth grade student attitudes toward and achievement in mathematics. Dissertation Abstracts International. 1987 Dec vol 48(6-a) 1391.

Vilenskaya-L. Firewalking and beyond. PSI Research. 1985 Jun vol 4(2) 89-109.

Vilenskaya-L. My view of psi in criminology: interview with Ron Nolan. PSI Research. 1984 Sep-dec vol 3(3-4) 118-130.

Vokey-J-R. Read-J-D. Subliminal messages: between the devil and the media. American Psychologist. 1985 Nov vol 40(11) 1231-1239.

Voronin-L-G. Novikov-P-P. Volkov-E-V. Dubinin-V-A. Formation and development of temporary connections with participation of perceived and nonperceived sound stimuli. Zhurnal Vysshei Nervnoi Deyatel'Nosti. 1984 Vol 34(5) 855-860.

Vroon-P-A. From radio metaphor to computer metaphor: publication trends in psychology. Gedrag: Tijdschrift voor Psychologie. 1985 Vol 13(6) 1-9.

Weinberger-J. Comment on Robert Fudin's paper "subliminal psychodynamic activation: Mommy and I are not yet one."Perceptual & Motor Skills.1986 Dec vol 63(3) 1232-1234.

West-G-N. The effects of auditory subliminal psychodynamic activation on state anxiety. Dissertation Abstracts International. 1985 Jul vol 46(1-b) 319.

West-D-J. Evidence for the paranormal: gains and losses. Journal of the Society for Psychical Research. 1987 Jan vol 54(806) 1-15.

Westerlundh-B. On reading subliminal sentences: a psychodynamic activation study. Psychological Research Bulletin, Lund U. 1986 Vol 26(10) 18 p.

Westerlundh-B. Personal organization of the visual field: a study of ambient to focal reports of threatening stimuli. Arch-Psychol (Frankf). 1983. 135(1). P 17-35.

Westerlundh-B. Subliminal influence on imagery: two exploratory experiments. Psychological Research Bulletin, Lund U. 1985 Vol 25(6-7) 31 p.

Westerlundh-B-E. Terjestam-Y-C. Psychodynamic effects of subliminal verbal messages on tachistoscopically presented interpersonal stimuli. Psychological Research Bulletin, Lund U. 1987 Vol 27(3) 21 p.

Yager-E-K. Subliminal therapy: utilizing the unconscious mind. Medical Hypnoanalysis Journal. 1987 Dec vol 2(4) 138-147.

Appendix E

Bibliography

Here is a list of books and other selected materials that we used in our research for this book and thought you'd find of interest. Some of these works and authors are referred to in the text, others are listed here as additional reading for the energetic researcher.

If we missed a work that you're familiar with and think should be included here to help us and others with further research, please let us know by writing to us care of the publisher or the Institute for Subliminal Studies.

Abraham, Suzanne, and Llewellyn-Jones, Derek. *Eating Disorders*. New York: Oxford University Press, 1987.

Bloom, Pamela. "Soul Music." *New Age Journal*, March/April 1987; 58-63.

Branden, Barbara. *The Passion of Ayn Rand.* New York: Doubleday & Company, 1986.

Branden, Nathaniel. *Honoring the Self.* Los Angeles: Jeremy P. Tarcher, 1983.

Branden, Nathaniel. *If You Could Hear What I Cannot Say.* New York: Bantam Books, 1983.

Branden, Nathaniel. *To See What I See and Know What I Know.* New York: Bantam Books, 1986.

Branden, Nathaniel. *The Psychology of High Self-Esteem.* Audio cassette program. Chicago: Nightingale-Conant Corporation, 1986.

Callahan, Roger J. *Five-Minute Phobia Cure.* Wilmington, DE: Enterprise Publishing, 1985.

Clark, Ronald W. *Einstein.* New York: World Publishing Company, 1971.

Cousins, Norman. *Anatomy of an Illness.* New York: W. W. Norton & Company, 1979.
Cousins, Norman. *Human Options.*

New York: W. W. Norton & Company, 1981.

Cousins, Norman. *Head First: The Biology of Hope*. New York: E. P. Dutton, 1989.

Diamond, John. *Your Body Doesn't Lie*. New York: Warner Books, 1979.

Diamond, John. *Speech, Language, and the Power of the Breath*. Valley Cottage, NY: Archaeus Press, 1979.

Dixon, N. F. *Preconscious Processing*. Chichester, England: Wiley, 1981.

Dixon, N. F. *Subliminal Perception*. London: McGraw-Hill, 1971.

Ellis, Albert. *Reason and Emotion in Psychotherapy*. New York: Lyle Stuart, 1962.

Ellis, Albert, and Harper, Robert A. *A Guide to Rational Living*. New Jersey: Prentice-Hall, 1961.

Epictetus. *The Discourses of Epictetus*. Translated by George Long. Chicago: Vol. 12, Britannica, Great Books, 1952.

Erickson, Milton H., and Rossi, Ernest L. *Experiencing Hypnosis*. New York: Irvington Publishers, 1981.

Freud, Sigmund. *The Major Works of Sigmund Freud*. Chicago: Vol. 54, Britannica, Great Books, 1952.

Genkina, O. A., and Shostakovich, G. S. *Soviet Neurology and Psychiatry*. Moscow: Nauka Publishers, 1983. The authors are associated with the V. P. Serbsky All-Union Scientific Research Institute of General and Forensic Psychiatry, Moscow.

Hill, Napoleon. *Think and Grow Rich*. New York: Fawcett Crest, 1963.

James, William. *The Principles of Psychology*. Chicago: Vol. 53, Britannica, Great Books, 1952.

Jerome, John. "The Body Athletic." *Esquire,* March 1980; 17-18.

Jung, Carl G. *Memories, Dreams, Reflections.* Translated by Richard and Clara Winston. New York: Random House, 1965.

Key, Wilson B. *Media Sexploitation.* New York: New American Library, 1972.

Key, Wilson B. *Subliminal Seduction.* New York: New American Library, 1972.

Koestler, Arthur. *The Act of Creation.* New York: Macmillan Company, 1964.

Lesser, Gershon M. *Growing Younger.* Los Angeles: Jeremy P. Tarcher, 1987.

Locke, Steven, and Colligan, Douglas. *The Healer Within.* New York: New American Library, 1986.

Luce, Gay G., and Segal, Julius. *Sleep.* New York: Lancer Books, 1966.

Maslow, Abraham H. *Dominance, Self-Esteem, Self-Actualization.* Monterey, CA: Brooks/Cole Publishing Company, 1973.

Maslow. Abraham H. *Motivation and Personality.* New York: Harper, 1955.

Perls, Frederick, Hefferline, Ralph E., and Goodman, Paul. *Gestalt Therapy.* New York: Dell Publishing, 1951.

Restak, Richard. *The Brain.* New York: Bantam Books, 1984.

Shulman, Lee, and Taylor, Joan Kennedy. *When to See a Psychologist.* Los Angeles: Nash Publishing Company, 1970.

Simonton, O. Carl. *Getting Well.* Audio cassette program. Los Angeles: Audio Renaissance Tapes, 1987.

Taylor, Eldon. *Subliminal Communication.* Salt Lake City: Just Another Reality, 1988.

Index

"Abundant Energy," 61, 77
Activator, subliminal, 114
Advertising, subliminal techniques in, 15–16
Affirmations, 107, 170–71
  defined, 106
  in hypnosis, 110
  principle behind, 100
Affirmations, subliminal, 107–9, 112
  effective grammar in, 109, 110, 116
  number of, 116, 118, 119–20
  subconscious and, 109
Aidlin, Joe, xiii
Alpha state, 40, 41, 42
Alphasonics, xiii
Anatomy of an Illness, 94, 96, 246
"Anti-Diet Weight Control Program," 135
Applied kinesiology (muscle testing), 143, 145–49, 151–53
Ariam, Sima, 114
Audiotapes, subliminal. *See* Subliminals
Auditory person, 120. *See also*

Communication groups

Awareness
  conscious, 36, 141
  objective, 39
  states of, 41
  subjective, 39

Background sounds, 128–29
Balanced needs, 203
Beliefs, basic, 53–59, 197
Bergman, Bill, xiii
Beta state, 41, 42
Brain wave
  activity, change in, 20
  patterns, 40–42
  state, optimal, 129
Branden, Barbara, 51, 246
Branden, Nathaniel, xi, 64, 65, 246
Brodsky, Nancy, xiii
Bryant-Tuckett, Rose, 112
Budzynski, Thomas, 42

Callahan, Roger, xiii, 246
Calories, 190–92
Chakras, 132
Chemotherapy study, 92–93
Clark, Ronald, 51, 246
Communication groups, 118
Compact disks, 44–45
Conscious awareness, 36, 141
Conscious mind, 26

Control group, 113
Cousins, Norman, x, xix, 93, 94, 96, 246, 247
Cover sounds, 125. *See also* Masking sounds
Crime prevention, 161
Cycles per second, 40, 41

"Daddy" phrase, 115–16
Decibels, 37, 39
Deformations, 107
Delta state, 41
Derycz, Peter, xiii
Diamond, John, xiii, 127, 148, 247
Digitized sound, 45
Dominant satisfier (food as), 202, 204

Einstein: The Life and Times, 51, 246
Epictetus, 3, 248
Erickson, Milton H., xiii, 88, 91, 110, 248
Exams. *See* Test taking
Experience + Response = Outcome, 52
Experiencing Hypnosis: Therapeutic Approaches to Altered States, 91, 248
Experiments, subliminal. *See* Research; Testing

Fat, excess, 190
Fatigue, combatting, 61–62, 77
Federal Communications Commission, 141, 165
Feeling people, 118
Food
  cycles, 199–200
  as dominant satisfier, 202, 204
  plan, 201–2
  as reward, 197–98
Ford, Henry, 103
Freud, Sigmund, 5, 248

Garland, Gloria, xii
Gillies, Jerry, xii
Goodheart, George, 145
Gordon, Nancy, xii
Gottlieb, Larry, xii
Greenberger, Feris M., xi
Growing Younger: Nutritional Rejuvenation for People Over Forty, 34, 249

Head First: The Biology of Hope, 96, 247
Healing
  mind and, 93
  music and, 134
Hill, Napoleon, 43, 248
Hovsepian and Quatman, subliminal research of, 17–19

Human Options, 93, 247
Hypnosis
  affirmations in, 110
  mind/body interaction and, 88–91

If You Could Hear What I Cannot Say, 65, 246
Imagery, subliminal, 120
Infotrieve Systems, xiii
Inside Edge Group, xiv
Institute for Subliminal Studies, 29, 46–47, 183, 209–10

"Joy of Learning," 49

Key, Wilson, 17, 18, 167, 249
Kinesthetic person, 120. *See also* Communication groups
Kirzhner, Alexander, xii, 128, 129

Laws
  flyers, 157
  junk mail, 156
  privacy, 155
  subliminals, 155, 164–66
  subliminals, availability of scripts, 167–68
  subliminals, defining the scope of, 166–67
  truth-in-packaging, 121, 167
Learning, subliminal, 6, 101

Lesser, Gershon M., xi, 34, 35. 249
Lie detectors, 144, 150
Lippman, Susannah, xiii
Listening people, 118
Lower theta state, 41
Lozanov, Georgi, 129–30

Mahr, Shelley, xiv
Masking sounds, 38
  features of, 125, 126
  impact on chakras of, 132
  impact on human body of, 127
  as primary attribute of tapes, 129–30
  varieties of, 124–25
  volume of, 133
Maslow, Abraham, xiii, 250
Messages
  inappropriate, 55
  verbal, 59
Messages, subliminal, 20, 21. *See also* Scripts, subliminal
  recording of, 44, 45–46
  speed of, 38, 40, 117
Mind/body interaction
  chemotherapy study and, 92–93
  demonstration of, in hypnosis, 88–91
Minimal perception, 21
"Mommy (and I are one)" phrase, 113–16

in Hebrew translation, 114–15
Muscle testing. *See* Applied kinesiology
Music
  benefits of, 130–31
  desirability of, as masking sound, 126, 132–33
  effect on the body of, 127–128
  healing with, 134
  sound patterns, 129–30

Negatives ("Don't"), 107–8
Neurolinguistic programming (NLP), 108, 110, 116
Neutral statement, 113
Nutrition. *See* Food; Weight control

Ohio State University, minimal-perception research at, 21
Oneness fantasy, 112–15

Pain-killing opiates (produced by the brain), 94–95
Parker, Kenneth, 114
The Passion of Ayn Rand, 51, 246
Perception, minimal, 21
Picnic experiment, 139–40
Pierce, Gordon, xiii
Placebo, 94, 95
Placebo effect of subliminals, 13, 95, 96–97, 159

Placebo tape, 96
Plato, 3
Plutarch, 3
Positive emotions, 43
Privacy, 155–58, 159–60
"The Psychology of High Self-Esteem," 64, 246
Pythagoras, 133–34

Quatman. *See* Hovsepian and Quatman
Queens College, New York, subliminal research at, 114

Radio broadcasts of subliminals, 22–23
Rand, Ayn, 51
Relaxation, inducing, 43–44
Relaxed state, 41, 42
Research, subliminal
 disagreements in, 136, 138–39
 duplicating results of, 17, 19
 negative results, 17–19, 20–21, 21–22
 permanence of results of, 80–81
 positive results, 112–13, 114, 114–15, 116
"Restful Night's Sleep," 77
Rossi, Ernest, 91, 248

Sales, increasing, 163–64
Scripts, negative, 102

Scripts, subliminal
  availability of, 120, 169
  decibel level of, 38
  effective elements of, 107–8, 119 (*see also* Affirmations)
  laws regarding, 167–68
  oneness fantasy in, 112–15
Seeing people, 118
Self-talk, 102, 107. *See also* Affirmations
Sentence-completion, 64–66
Shoplifting, reduction in, 160–61, 162
Siller, Jerome, 114
Silverman, Lloyd, 112, 115
Sleep, inducing, 77
Smiling (to increase energy), 150
Smoking, stopping, 60–61, 82, 87, 99, 159
Sound, digitized, 45
Sound patterns (musical), 129, 130
Sounds, subliminal, 38. *See also* Masking sounds; Music
Stereo, subliminals recorded in, 44
Stimulation, subliminal, 33
  of alcoholics, 20
  undirected 33
Stress, 58, 144–45
Stress management, 62–63, 67–69, 70–71

Subconscious, 36, 57
  ability of, to understand subliminals, 40, 59, 117, 169
  functioning of, 26–27, 108, 109
Subliminal, 36, 39
Subliminal activator, 114
Subliminal learning, 6, 101
Subliminal mind, 109
Subliminal products
  advertising of, 14
  audiotapes (*see* Subliminals)
  varieties of, existing, 178–79
  varieties of, proposed, 179–81
Subliminal Seduction, 18, 167, 249
Subliminals. *See also individual topics* (Smoking; Test taking; etc.)
  defined, 35–36
  defining, in law, 166–67
  imagery of, 120
  judging effectiveness of, 83–84, 138–39, 152–53
  limits to effectiveness of, 60–62, 71–72, 73, 162
  permanence of effects of, 79–81
  personalized, 111
  principles of, 13
  used without knowledge or consent, 139–40, 158–59, 160–61, 164
Substimulation, 129

Sugar, 198–99
Sugar test, 151
Supraliminal, 39

Tachistoscope, 112–13
Taylor, Joan Kennedy, xi, 250
Test taking (exams), 31–32, 49–50, 82–83
Testing clear, strong, and weak, 145–50, 151, 152–53
Testing subliminals, 136
 with academic controls (*see* Research)
 without academic controls, 22–23, 96, 139–40, 158–59, 160–61
Theta state, 40, 41
Think and Grow Rich , 43, 248
The 30-Day Renewable Marriage: Keeping Romance Alive, xvi
Thoughts, Behavior, Feelings, the interrelationship of, 74
Thresholds, subliminal, 36–38, 39
Thymus, 150
Tomatis, Alfred A., 130, 131
Truth-in-packaging laws, 121, 167

Unbalanced needs, 204
Unconscious, 36
Undirected subliminal stimulation, 33

University of Northern Colorado, subliminal research at, 20–21
University of Wisconsin, subliminal research at, 21–22
Upper theta state, 40, 41

Visual person, 120. *See also* Communication groups
Voice portions of subliminals, 45–46
Voices of English grammar, 110

Weight control (weight loss)
  nutrition and, 188–92
  physiology of, 186–88
  psychology of, 56–57, 193–98, 199
  subliminals and, 84–85, 123–24, 135, 185, 207
"Winning at Exams," 49, 82

Xavier University, subliminal research at, 17–19

Your Body Doesn't Lie, 127, 247

Other Titles Available From:
InfoBooks
P.O. Box 1018
Santa Monica, California 90406
213-394-4102, Fax 394-2603 • 1-800-669-0409

Please send me the following books			
No.	Title	Unit Price	Extended Price
	Subliminal: The New Channel	$ 9.95	
	Your Best Interest	$ 9.95	
	The Tao of Programming	$ 7.95	
	The Zen of Programming	$ 7.95	
	Computer Parables	$ 7.95	
	The Writer's Pocket Almanack	$ 7.95	
	Poster Catalog	FREE	
	Book Catalog	FREE	

Taxes: In California please add 6.75% sales tax.
Shipping: $1.50 first book; $1.00 each additional book for surface mail.
$.2.50 first book; $2.00 each additional book for first class.
Commercial orders will be shipped UPS surface.

Ship To:

Name_____

Company_____

Address_____

City_____State_____Zip_____

Telephone _____

Payment

Payment must accompany all orders. For international shipments please add $2.00 and make checks payable in U.S. dollars drawn on a U.S. bank, or an international money order.

Thank You For Your Order

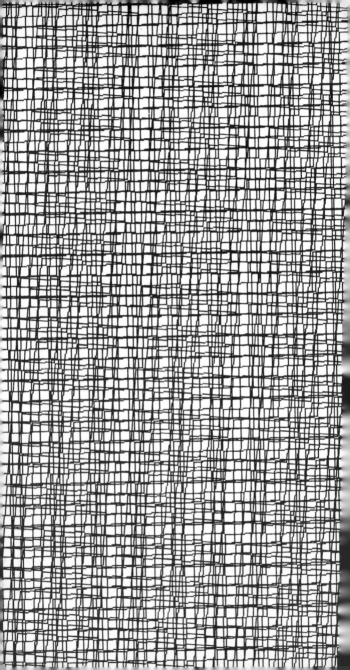